# THE ABUNDANT KINGDOM:

## YOUR PROSPERITY GUARANTEED

# VINCE AMAECHI

**Xulon** PRESS

# CONTENTS

—⟨∿∿⟩—

# DEDICATION

———❧❧❧———

*I am dedicating this book to my grand daughter,
Shekinah. She brings the glory of God with her
whenever she comes to visit and I like the way she
says, "Hello gan-dad." I think it's the way she says
it; which you can't visualise on these pages.*

# Acknowledgements

———∿∿∿———

I would like to acknowledge with gratitude the patience and painstaking manner with which my editor, Pastor Israel Emmanuel, of *Emmanuel Publishing Services*, has applied to thorough proof-reading and editing of this book. I want to thank those of you who have read Vol. 1 and shared with me how much you have enjoyed reading it, and why it is imperative that the rest of the volumes are published soon.

I would also like to thank Miss Jade Astell and Miss Beryl Nartey, my secretaries, who did the tedious job of deciphering my handwriting from the manuscripts and typing them out to what you are reading today.

I am deeply indebted to Dr. Soji Baikie, Area Secretary, Overseas Fellowship of Nigerian Christians (OFNC) UK, London Branch, for making out time from his busy schedule to read this book and write the foreword. His comments and observations are highly appreciated.

Finally, I want to thank my wife, Ogoma, and my children, Chinoge, Daberechi, Obuineke, Ngozi and Ozioma, for always being there for me and giving me the strength and morale boost that was needed for doing these writings.

Thank you all and may God bless you.

# FOREWORD

—◈—

T his great piece of work, *The Abundant
Kingdom*, is the second in the *Luke For
Absolute Beginners Series*. As with the first book,
*The Son Of Man Has Come*, Dr. Vince Amaechi
takes us through an in-depth, verse-by-verse study
and in doing so, highlights important areas of prac-
tical application to our daily lives.

The author is a man of great capacity: husband,
father, grandfather, counsellor, preacher and teacher;
and for those who know him well, the book bears
many hallmarks of the person of Dr. Amaechi. He is
passionate about teaching the word and his approach
is effective in *"giving light to the readers and understanding to the simple"* (Psalm 119:130).

After a night of fruitless endeavour, the fishermen
obeyed Jesus, cast their net in the lake and 'caught a
multiple of fishes'. But shortly after bringing their
ships to land, they forsook all and followed him.

There are many people around the world who
have come to the conclusion that material posses-
sions do not lead to fulfilment. This book will inspire
and encourage you; it will point you to Yeshua, the

source and giver of abundant life. I commend it to you.

- **Dr Soji Baikie**
*General Practitioner & Area Secretary*
*Overseas Fellowship of Nigerian Christians*
*(OFNC)*
*London Branch*

# INTRODUCTION

---

I n *The Abundant Kingdom*, the second volume of my Luke commentaries, we will be getting to know the character and personality of the Lord Yeshua more deeply.

We will see how much God cares for His children and also see Him as the Greatest Physician who knows us through and through as well as inside out. He knows what we are made of and is able to heal us physically as well as spiritually.

We will also see a compassionate God who is touched by the weakness of our physical frame. Because of this, He instituted a day of rest for us to rejuvenate our bodies. He set up the Sabbath for man and is *also* Lord of the Sabbath.

We will learn, in the first instance, that God's ways are not our ways; that His ways are far beyond our imagination and logic, and secondly, that He knows the end from the beginning.

God knows what is good for us even when we do not recognise it ourselves. Most of the time we become impatient with Him, but in this study we will learn the importance of being patient with God because His plans for us are for good and not of evil; plans to give us an expected end.

It would help if you have read Volume 1, *The Son Of Man Has Come*. It is always good to start something from the very beginning, so I would recommend that you do that. However, the style and simplicity of the series makes it easy for anyone to appreciate and enjoy reading the series from whatever volume they choose.

Volume one took us through the prophecy of the coming of the Lord Yeshua, the Son of Man, to His actual arrival. In this volume, we will continue to explore how we can go deep-sea fishing with Him and experience the bumper catch that comes with getting to know Him better. We we learn how to trust the word of God implicitly, to send out the WORD that can accomplish our desire in the will of God, and to do exploits in the name of the Lord.

In the end, this volume will explore who this man Yeshua is and consider His claim that He is the resurrection and the life who rules and reigns in God's Abundant Kingdom.

# LUKE CHAPTER 5

# 1

# LET'S GO FISHING

———◦◦◦———

## Luke 5:1-16

[1]And it came to pass, that, as the people pressed upon him to hear the word of God, he stood by the lake of Gennesaret, [2]And saw two ships standing by the lake: but the fishermen were gone out of them, and were washing their nets. [3]And he entered into one of the ships, which was Simon's, and prayed him that he would thrust out a little from the land. And he sat down, and taught the people out of the ship. [4]Now when he had left speaking, he said unto Simon, Launch out into the deep, and let down your nets for a draught. [5]And Simon answering said unto him, Master, we have toiled all the night, and have taken nothing: nevertheless at thy word I will let down the net. [6]And when they had this done, they inclosed a great multitude of fishes: and their net brake. [7]And they beckoned unto their partners, which were in the other ship, that they should come and help

them. And they came, and filled both the ships, so that they began to sink. [8]When Simon Peter saw it, he fell down at Jesus' knees, saying, Depart from me; for I am a sinful man, O Lord. [9]For he was astonished, and all that were with him, at the draught of the fishes which they had taken: [10]And so was also James, and John, the sons of Zebedee, which were partners with Simon. And Jesus said unto Simon, Fear not; from henceforth thou shalt catch men. [11]And when they had brought their ships to land, they forsook all, and followed him. [12]And it came to pass, when he was in a certain city, behold a man full of leprosy: who seeing Jesus fell on his face, and besought him, saying, Lord, if thou wilt, thou canst make me clean. [13]And he put forth his hand, and touched him, saying, I will: be thou clean. And immediately the leprosy departed from him. [14]And he charged him to tell no man: but go, and shew thyself to the priest, and offer for thy cleansing, according as Moses commanded, for a testimony unto them. [15]But so much the more went there a fame abroad of him: and great multitudes came together to hear, and to be healed by him of their infirmities. [16]And he withdrew himself into the wilderness, and prayed.

**(Luke 5:1-16)**

F ishermen, those who fish for a living, go far out into the sea. Amateur fishermen or those for whom fishing is a hobby stay by the bank of the river. The professionals use different kinds of instruments and they catch all sorts of fish.

Here, we learn from the Lord Yeshua Himself (the Master Fisherman) that if you want to fish for real, you have to go beyond the shallow waters and away from the shores or edge of the river. You need to go deep into the sea where the fish are.

Verse 1

Straight away from verse one, we notice that everything the Lord did was dependent on the Word. Many people today run to church or to the minister, expecting a miracle even before hearing one word of what the minister has to teach or what he or she believes. To such people, the word of God is irrelevant, they want their miracles and they want it now.

In this passage (just as in many other passages), the Lord starts His ministration by preaching and teaching the people. The more He taught, the more He built faith in them to understand and believe that He is capable of doing what He said He would. Surely, *faith comes by hearing; and hearing the word of God* (Romans 10:17).

Oh, how I wish we would all follow the Lord's example, even as we minister to people who come to see us or attend our meetings! The problem is that everyone is trying hard to please their 'clients' rather than please the Lord. Most ministers I have seen or heard will start praying "power" miracle prayers even before they have fully heard what the problem is from the 'client'. It is all a show off to prove that they have "a powerful anointing for miracles."

I have heard miracle workers on TV and radio start shouting prayers for miracles, signs and wonders even before the caller had finished speaking; they would not let the caller get a word in edgeways.

In this passage, while the people were still meditating on what He had taught them, the Lord performed a miracle. Since they were still filled with the power of the Word, they could handle it because they knew the heart and source of the miracle.

Verse 2

The fishermen and the workers had finished work for the day (or so they thought), but the Lord had other ideas.

Many of us are at that level right now. We think we have finished. "It's not working out; let's pack it up and go home."

Then again, it could be that you are one of those who have done everything that needs to be done. During your youth and during the day, you have done everything. You have been there, done that, and won the T-shirt! It is now late, you think. It is time to hang up the gloves and have a rest. There's nothing wrong with that. Only keep your ears open, because the Lord might be saying, "Cast your net on the other side."

The Lord Yeshua says, "It may be late in the evening; you may be clearing up to go home and have a rest from the great work you've done in the past. But please put out your net a bit more. This time, try going in a bit deeper. You might just surprise yourself. Move away from the land. Move away from your comfort zone. You might surprise just yourself."

Verses 3-4

In every situation, we see the Lord teaching something deep and profound. "Simon Peter, let's go fishing: deep sea fishing." Put your nets out into the deep for a catch. Venture out a little bit more than you are doing at the moment in whatever it is that you are doing, especially in your spiritual walk with God. Strive to go a bit deeper than the normal shallow end.

Verse 5

### *Excuses*

Just like Peter, we all have excuses. Some of those excuses come from what we think we know. Thus, our experiences easily become the hindrance blocking our way from listening and obeying the Lord's command.

Past experience, professional experience, social experience and academic experience all play a part in hindering us from a close relationship with the Lord.

Peter was a professional fisherman who had been fishing all his youth. If anyone should know where to catch fish, he should. On the other hand, Yeshua was "a carpenter's son" who probably had never gone fishing before. What would He know about where to catch fish? Professional experience would have been a big hindrance for Peter, but thank God he didn't let it stop him from having a deeper relationship with the Lord or learning more from Him.

Which one of these is stopping you from going deep sea fishing with the Lord and reaping your great harvest? Listen to the Lord Yeshua today. One word from Him can change your life for good.

Verses 6-7

One of the biggest problems we have as human beings is pride. Pride comes up especially when someone comes and starts talking to us about our business or our profession, as if they know anything about it or even better. The smirk on our faces and the sarcasm in our words stops us from listening or even recognising that they may be making sense or may even have a point. We brush them off. The worst of all is that the professional in us would find it hard to give in, apologise or repent. Peter repented.

Repentance is wonderful. It enables you to receive your haul of treasure from the Lord; too great for few to handle. When the Lord blesses the humble, He blesses him to overflowing. Sharing becomes inevitable, more hands are busy and more wealth is created.

Verses 8-9

Signs and wonders are given to us so we may worship God more than we have ever done before. They make us marvel at the power and glory of God, not of man. They give us more reverence and adoration for the awesomeness of God. Miracles, signs and wonders are not given to us so that we can glorify the person whom God has used to do the miraculous signs.

Verses 10 -11

When you are blessed, your partners will be blessed too. You learn to share. Your partners, other churches and ministries around you, get to feel the influence of your growth and not your power or politics. Combined hands and effort will mean more souls saved into the kingdom. Burdens shared will be burdens halved.

Here we see the principles of increase that the Lord was teaching. And when you get to know Him through your caring and sharing, you cannot help but worship Him even more.

Verses 12-13

Here is one of those special moments in the Gospel of Luke that tells us exactly why God inspired him to write a Gospel for the Gentiles, the outcasts, the poor and the needy.

Before the coming of the Lord Yeshua, good news about worshiping God and being acceptable to God was reserved for the well-groomed Jew who had neither spot nor blemish. Those who did not fit into that neat category were outcasts. Lepers were the worst of such outcasts. They lived away from the normal society and were classed as unclean. They did not eat, drink, shop, sleep or touch like normal people. They could not come near other people who were supposedly holy; neither did they come close to places of worship. They had bells around their bodies, which they rang to warn people that they were approaching, lest they contaminate the holy people. If they did not do this, they could be stoned to death.

That was the grim picture of life for the poor, the oppressed and the outcasts before the advent of the Gospel of grace in which Luke received his salvation and could not hold back from explaining it to the 'Most Excellent Theophilus'.

We learn from this leper that while there is life, there is hope in God. No matter how grim and impossible things may seem, as long as you still have one second, God can turn things around. All you have to do is have faith in God. Even to the last minute, He will show up and He will be God.

As for the leper, could he dare to ask? Could he let this chance of being healed pass him by? *"Do I trust him enough? Would he make a mockery of me? Would he care to talk to me? The priests and the Pharisee would not see me, let alone talk to me. He is different. Would he do it for me, as I hear he had been doing for other sick people? Will he or will he not?"*

In his mind he was saying, "I know your capabilities. No one else can do what you do. Only you can make me whole." He went near him and actually touched him. What faith! What bravery! The Lord responded. "I am willing, be made clean."

Here we learn that contrary to our views of God, He is always willing to make us clean, draw us close to Himself, touch us and be our friend. God is willing and always ready to come close and be *your* friend.

Verses 14-15 teaches us about doing first things first. Thank God you are now converted. Thank God you are now born again. You are no longer a member of the kingdom of darkness; no longer an outcast to the kingdom of God. You are now translated into the new world of the kingdom of light. But first things first; you need debriefing and the renewing of your mind before you can take on the serious business of being a disciple.

First, you need to go to a pastor, a minister, a teacher, a mentor or an older person in the Lord for your debriefing and training on how to re-enter life in normal society and how to operate in a different kingdom. Tell others; tell the congregation where you have been and where the Lord has rescued you from.

We have seen examples of this in the past few decades when aid workers, journalists, peace envoys were kidnapped by terrorists. Upon release, they are taken to some special location by their country where they are debriefed and even taught what to say and how to respond in the new free society.

What the Lord was teaching us there is that whoever we may be, like the leper, we need cleaning up, debriefing with his word, and learning to stay clear of the enemy (lest he strikes again even before we can think of doing any big thing to follow the Lord). Also here, the Lord says, "Just live the life; don't worry about my fame. The news of what I have done for you will spread itself throughout the land."

Verse 16

Workaholics anonymous, beware! Too much work results in less time to pray. The Lord Yeshua took time off to rest. He took time out to pray. We all need to learn from that.

*You need the word.*
*You need the Lord.*
*You need to work.*
*You need the rest.*
*So,*
*Let's go fishing,*
*deep sea fishing.*

# 2

# YESHUA, THE GREAT PHYSICIAN

———◈◈◈———

## Luke 5:17-39

[17]And it came to pass on a certain day, as he was teaching, that there were Pharisees and doctors of the law sitting by, which were come out of every town of Galilee, and Judaea, and Jerusalem: and the power of the Lord was present to heal them. [18]And, behold, men brought in a bed a man which was taken with a palsy: and they sought means to bring him in, and to lay him before him. [19]And when they could not find by what way they might bring him in because of the multitude, they went upon the housetop, and let him down through the tiling with his couch into the midst before Jesus. [20]And when he saw their faith, he said unto him, Man, thy sins are forgiven thee. [21]And the scribes and the Pharisees began to reason, saying, Who is this which

speaketh blasphemies? Who can forgive sins, but God alone? [22]But when Jesus perceived their thoughts, he answering said unto them, What reason ye in your hearts? [23]Whether is easier, to say, Thy sins be forgiven thee; or to say, Rise up and walk? [24]But that ye may know that the Son of man hath power upon earth to forgive sins, (he said unto the sick of the palsy,) I say unto thee, Arise, and take up thy couch, and go into thine house. [25]And immediately he rose up before them, and took up that whereon he lay, and departed to his own house, glorifying God. [26]And they were all amazed, and they glorified God, and were filled with fear, saying, We have seen strange things today. [27]And after these things he went forth, and saw a publican, named Levi, sitting at the receipt of custom: and he said unto him, Follow me. [28]And he left all, rose up, and followed him. [29]And Levi made him a great feast in his own house: and there was a great company of publicans and of others that sat down with them. [30]But their scribes and Pharisees murmured against his disciples, saying, Why do ye eat and drink with publicans and sinners? [31]And Jesus answering said unto them, They that are whole need not a physician; but they that are sick. [32]I came not to call the righteous, but sinners to repentance. [33]And they said unto him, Why do the disciples of John fast often, and make prayers, and likewise the disciples of the Pharisees; but thine eat and drink? [34]And he said unto them, Can ye make the children of the bridechamber fast, while the bridegroom is with them? [35]But the days will come, when the bridegroom shall be taken away from them, and then shall they fast in those days. [36]And he spake also a parable unto them; No man putteth a piece of a new garment upon an old; if otherwise, then both the new maketh a rent, and the piece that was taken out of the new agreeth not with the old. [37]And no man putteth new wine into old bottles; else the new wine will burst the bottles, and be spilled, and the bottles shall perish. [38]But new wine must be put into new bottles; and both are preserved. [39]No man also having drunk old wine straightway desireth new: for he saith, The old is better.

### (Luke 5:17-39)

In this chapter, I want us to study the Lord Yeshua as our Great Physician. Simply put, the word 'physician' means 'doctor'; one who diagnoses and cures people of their ailments.

Can you imagine a man getting up one morning and going to the doctor's surgery, though he is perfectly alright and nothing is wrong with him?

He walks into the doctor's room.

Doctor says: *"Yes, Mr Blah. What can I do for you?"*

Mr Blah: *"Nothing."*

Doctor: *"Well, why are you here?"*
Mr Blah: *"No, just wanted to see a doctor."*
Doctor: *"Well, what's wrong with you?"*
Mr Blah: *"Nothing."*
The doctor responds:
*"Next! This man doesn't need a doctor. There's nothing wrong with him. He's wasting my time."*

Only the sick need a physician. However, people can sometimes be ill without even realising it or knowing what's wrong with them. Sometimes people are ill but they refuse to see a doctor. Others see a doctor but refuse to take the prescribed medication, thinking the sickness will just disappear.

There are good doctors who will take time with you and check you out thoroughly before prescribing the right medication. There are bad doctors too who do not have time for you. Before you can finish explaining how you feel, they have already written the prescription. They are too busy. They have hundreds to see and yet see none of them properly.

Not like the Lord Yeshua our Great Physician! He has enough time for all classes of people, especially those who have acknowledged their need for healing. Even those who have not realised how sick they are receive healing from the kindness of the Great Physician.

He makes us understand that there is a connection between illnesses and sin. The connection may not be clear to you and I, but the Lord says so and encourages us to stay away from all appearances of sin and evil. But if we recognise any sin or sickness in our lives, we should come to Him boldly and He will heal us because He is our Healer and Great Physician.

Verse 17 says that as He was preaching and teaching, the power in the word was present to heal the people. The power to heal is in the word of God. If anyone tells you otherwise, they are lying to you.

Verses 18-19

At this particular teaching/healing session, there were various categories of people from all walks of life; the great and the good, the poor and the needy, the learned and the not-so-well learned. There were also the experts, including the doctors and teachers of the law.

A group of men had a friend who needed healing. They knew the Lord Yeshua was never stationary; He moved from place to place as he wished. If they missed Him at that moment, they knew they might not see him for a long time, and their friend might never receive the healing he so desperately needed. Love for their disabled friend compelled them to do an extraordinary thing to get into the presence of the Lord.

The Bible tells us that love covers a multitude of sins. In other words, there are things that you could do ordinarily that would get you into a lot of trouble, but when it's done in love and compassion, you could almost 'get away with murder.'

It is like what David did in the Old Testament out of compassion for his starving men (Matthew 12:3-4) He entered the house of God, went straight to the altar and took the consecrated shewbread that was meant only for the priests. He took it, ate it and even gave some to his fighting men who were neither anointed nor consecrated.

The Lord Yeshua was explaining to the people that the reason God overlooked that "sin" at that time was because He saw David's compassion for his men. Ordinarily, David (a man after God's heart), would not have blatantly flouted the law just to eat the holy bread. Here also, in the story of the man with disability and his friends, we see that no one is completely hopeless or helpless in life, especially if they put their trust in God. Most of the time, what people around us need is a little bit of TLC (Tender Loving Care).

The men in the story were late to the meeting. I guess some of the people reading this may be like them, always going late to meetings and expecting to get good seats, a good view or a good reception when they arrive! If this is one habit you have, ask God to help you beat it!

Others were there before them but they wanted the front position meant for people who were early. They tried everything but the crowd would not make room for them. Everyone wanted to see the Lord for themselves. Nonetheless, they desperately needed the Lord to intervene on behalf of their friend before he passed them by.

Their attitude and efforts said, "Whatever it takes, we are here for you. Never mind the roof; you are more precious than the roof. We will pay the owner of the house for damages later. All we want is for you to get better."

What friendship! I wonder if this kind of sacrificial friendship still exists in our communities today.

What a feeling of overwhelming gratitude we feel when others make extra effort on our behalf and say, "Whatever it takes. . . "!

They needed an "open door" before the Lord but it was not forth coming, so they started with a "breakthrough". They had great faith in the Lord; so they got from him what they wanted. Their faith touched God and he said to them, "Whatever it was, your sins are forgiven you."

> [20]And when he saw their faith, he said unto him, Man, thy sins are forgiven thee. [21]And the scribes and the Pharisees began to reason, saying, Who is this which speaketh blasphemies? Who can forgive sins, but God alone?

**(Luke 5:20,21)**

Verses 20-21

God did His business for the man, irrespective of what people would say. He healed him, regardless of opposition. God will fight your battles no matter the opposition to your case. He will prove your adversaries wrong by sorting out your situation in your favour.

The Lord declared to the watching crowd that he could create and make things happen and that he could speak things into being that were not in existence. He showed them that he was God, the God that can make impossibilities possible.

Verses 22-24

In these verses, we learn the hard truth that the Lord knows our thoughts. He knows our hearts and minds even when he is not present with us physically. Many times we think like the Pharisees and say in our hearts, "He does not know what we're thinking; he does not know what is going on."

It is foolish to think that way because the Bible tells us that only a fool says in his heart, "There is no God," presumably thinking he can hide his thoughts from the all-seeing God.

Verse 25

Immediately, the sick man got up. His sins were forgiven and he was healed - to the amazement of all the people. *"There is a connection,"* Jesus seemed to show, *"between sin and sickness; you may not know it but whichever way you want me to handle it – I am equal to the task. I can say, 'Get up and go home', 'Be healed' or 'Your sins are forgiven you'. I can do it whichever way I choose."*

Dear friend, the Lord can forgive your sins and also heal your spirit, soul and body.

Verse 26

As mentioned earlier, miracles are meant to present to us the awesomeness of God so that we can glorify Him. The people in the story shouted praises unto God. Many believed in the Lord Yeshua that he was the One; the Son of God.

Verses 27-28 reminds me of the days when I was a new convert and quite young in the Lord. Sometimes I get invited to birthday parties, only to get there and find out that the celebrants were celebrating the date of their new birth; the day they were born again.

Here we see Levi (Matthew), the tax collector, throwing a party, celebrating his new birth from the kingdom of 'the cheats' and deceit into the kingdom of light and love. Who could begrudge him for such an occasion, except the Pharisees and others who could not see the point of these celebrations and 'waste'? All that the Lord said was, "Come, follow me" and the rest was history.

The same thing has happened to billions of people around the world who heard the call, responded and followed the Lord. The Bible says he called them and they left everything and followed him. Whoever you may be, the call is still the same. Whatever your qualifications, whatever your business, whatever your experience, the Lord says, "Come follow me."

Verses 29-30

In these two verses, we see the Pharisees criticising the Lord for mingling and eating with publicans and sinners. For him to be a real upholder of the law, they expected him to separate himself from known sinners of the society. In those days, people were classified as sinners just because they did certain jobs.

It was obvious then, as it is even today, that if someone was a harlot, it was well-understood by society that such a person was a sinner. In the case of Levi, he was regarded as a sinner because of his occupation as a tax collector. (Can you imagine being seen as a sinner because you work for the tax office?).

Levi was automatically regarded as a sinner because he was employed by the Romans who were the enemy and oppressors of the Jews. He was employed to collect taxes from his own people (the Jews) for the Romans.

Even when the Jews were not so faithful and loyal to God as their leader and king, they always believed that Jews were not subject to any power other than God's. As far as they were concerned, anyone found on the side of the Romans or working for them could not possibly be on the side of God, hence a sinner.

What the Pharisees were saying to the Lord goes something like this; *"We know that birds of the same feather flock together. Sinners tend to tolerate other sinners like them. They eat, drink and party together in their own unclean environment. You seem to be so comfortable with them. It's either you are one of them or you're not really a holy man from God as you claim to be."*

This is where the Lord Yeshua used Luke to introduce us to another aspect of his ministry that the Pharisees did not understand. In a nutshell, the Lord was saying in verse 31, *"I am a physician, the Great Physician. As a matter of fact, the greatest physician you can ever meet. Whether you are sick physically or spiritually, I am equal to the task; I can heal them all. Whatever your sickness, whatever your sin, if you need me, I will be right there for you. I am the Great Physician and it's only those who are sick that seek a physician."*

The physician goes to those who need him. He cannot deal with them from a distance or at arm's length.

What the Lord was saying to the critics was that there are two kinds of sick people in the world: those who recognise their sins or sickness and realise they have the need for a physician, and those who are blind to these things and do not see the need for help.

On this particular occasion, the publicans, the harlots and other kinds of sinners had recognised their need and also recognised the Lord as the authentic healer. They asked him in because he is the Great Physician.

I don't know what your own status is as you read this book. I don't know what your sickness or disease may be. I don't know whether you are a sinner or not but God knows. The Pharisees were able to spot a sinner from a mile. However, the Bible says all have sinned and come short of the glory of God. That means ALL have sinned, including you and I. However, the gift of God is forgiveness and adoption into the family of God, plus eternal life through the Lord Yeshua, the Messiah.

Whatever your condition, (whether it is sin or sickness) you need the Lord Yeshua. He is the Great Physician who heals spirit, soul and body and has said, *"I will never leave you nor forsake you."*

When the critics did not succeed in bringing him down personally, they decided to turn their criticisms onto his disciples. Read verse 33 below:

[33]And they said unto him, Why do the disciples of John fast often, and make prayers, and likewise the disciples of the Pharisees; but thine eat and drink?

**(Luke 5:33)**

It seems to me that before the Lord gave his teaching on what real prayer and fasting is, and how private and personal it should be, everyone knew who was fasting and who was praying. It was mostly outward for everyone to notice. No wonder the critics were able to know that the disciples were neither fasting nor praying. They had not seen them wearing sackcloth and rent garments, which was the sign of mourning or fasting. They had not seen them at street corners and in the marketplaces praying, like John the Baptist and his disciples or the Pharisees and their disciples.

Take a look at Jesus' reply.

[34]And he said unto them, Can ye make the children of the bridechamber fast, while the bridegroom is with them? [35]But the days will come, when the bridegroom shall be taken away from them, and then shall they fast in those days.

From verses 34-35 the Lord explained to them why his disciples did not need to pray or fast while he was with them. His answer shows us one of those places in the Bible where the Lord subtly reveals to us that he was the Son of God, therefore that he was God. He gave them an illustration of himself being the bridegroom, that is, the master of the house and the disciples, his servants.

They could not be hungry or in want while God was there physically with them as the Owner of everything. If they needed anything, all they had to do was ask. God was with them; he loved them and dwelt among them. But time would come when he would not be with them, physically, then they would need to pray and fast for their needs and for all sorts of things.

From verses 36-39, he went further to explain that he was the new order, the new era, the new dispensation. He made it clear that he was teaching his disciples new ways of interpreting the Law and the Prophets. In other words, they were learning to put on new garments of God's own righteousness rather than the old garments of the Pharisees.

It would not be wise for him to mix up what he was trying to teach with the ways of the Pharisees. Doing so would be like wearing new clothes on top of the old wretched ones or like mixing old wine with new. It would be confusing and would not taste nice in the mouth. When you mix the new wine with the old, it will be all so mixed up that there will be no distinction. You would not be able to tell them apart.

<sup>36</sup>And he spake also a parable unto them; No man putteth a piece of a new garment upon an old; if otherwise, then both the new maketh a rent, and the piece that was taken out of

the new agreeth not with the old. [37]And no man putteth new wine into old bottles; else the new wine will burst the bottles, and be spilled, and the bottles shall perish. [38]But new wine must be put into new bottles; and both are preserved. [39]No man also having drunk old wine straightway desireth new: for he saith, The old is better.

# LUKE CHAPTER 6

## 3

# KEEPING THE SABBATH

———∽∿∿∾———

## Luke 6:1-11

As we read about the incidents and issues people discussed with the Lord, we will begin to see how the Lord gradually taught them, and that even though he did not come to abolish the law completely, there had to be a new way of looking at some of the laws. In some cases, he taught the people to go back to the beginning and find out why such a law was given in the first place. The law of keeping the Sabbath was one of them.

Keeping the Sabbath meant observing a day of rest from your works. To fully understand why the Sabbath was instituted, it would be necessary to read some scriptures relating to that. Two of such scriptures readily come to mind: Deuteronomy 5:14-15 and Luke 6:1-16.

> ¹⁴But the seventh day is the sabbath of the LORD thy God: in it thou shalt not do any work, thou, nor thy son, nor thy daughter, nor thy manservant, nor thy maidservant, nor

thine ox, nor thine ass, nor any of thy cattle, nor thy stranger that is within thy gates; that thy manservant and thy maidservant may rest as well as thou. [15]And remember that thou wast a servant in the land of Egypt, and that the LORD thy God brought thee out thence through a mighty hand and by a stretched out arm: therefore the LORD thy God commanded thee to keep the sabbath day.

### (Deuteronomy 5:14-15)

Simply put, the Sabbath is a day of rest from all our works. It is a day of meditation and reflection on what the Lord, our Deliverer, Sustainer and Defender has done for us. The Lord ordered this day of rest to enable the children of Israel to look after their bodies. They would be able to rest their bodies and also have time to reflect on who it was that gave them that rest and rescued them from slavery – God or the Egyptians.

Let's look at the next scripture.

[1]And it came to pass on the second sabbath after the first, that he went through the corn fields; and his disciples plucked the ears of corn, and did eat, rubbing them in their hands. [2]And certain of the Pharisees said unto them, Why do ye that which is not lawful to do on the sabbath days? [3]And Jesus answering them said, Have ye not read so much as this, what David did, when himself was an hungred, and they which were with him; [4]How he went into the house of God, and did take and eat the shewbread, and gave also to them that were with him; which it

is not lawful to eat but for the priests alone? [5]And he said unto them, That the Son of man is Lord also of the sabbath.

[6]And it came to pass also on another sabbath, that he entered into the synagogue and taught: and there was a man whose right hand was withered. [7]And the scribes and Pharisees watched him, whether he would heal on the sabbath day; that they might find an accusation against him. [8]But he knew their thoughts, and said to the man which had the withered hand, Rise up, and stand forth in the midst. And he arose and stood forth.

[9]Then said Jesus unto them, I will ask you one thing; Is it lawful on the sabbath days to do good, or to do evil? to save life, or to destroy it? [10]And looking round about upon them all, he said unto the man, Stretch forth thy hand. And he did so: and his hand was restored whole as the other. [11]And they were filled with madness; and communed one with another what they might do to Jesus.

### (Luke 6:1-11)

Jesus was passing through some corn fields with his disciples on a Sabbath day. They did three things: the disciples picked up ears of corn from the field, rubbed them with their hands to extract the grains and ate them to quench their hunger. They did that because they were hungry. They were not working or harvesting the farm.

Verse 2

The Pharisees accused them of doing things not lawful to be done on the Sabbath day. Reading through the scriptures about Sabbath, we can see that it clearly prohibits people working on the Sabbath day. But at this time, the time of Christ, the law has been expanded and embellished by the Pharisees to include, *"thou shalt not pick up a grain of corn, neither shalt thou rub it in thy hand, moreover thou shalt not eat it to quench thy hunger, it contravenes the Sabbath of the Lord." (my paraphrase)*.

So they said, "Why do you do what is not lawful to be done on the Sabbath?" By regarding what the disciples were doing as work (or rather, harvesting), they were overstating the text and interpreting it out of context. They were thus creating their own scriptures and laws and putting people back into bondage and slavery.

See how the Lord Yeshua answered them: *"Even if you don't know anything, have you not even read this portion of scripture...?"*

The Pharisees had great expectations of Jesus and his disciples; about what they should do and what they should not do, what they should know and what they should not know. At this point however, the Lord was turning the table round on the Pharisees and the critics. He implied that there were basic things the Pharisees should have known if they were worth their calling.

In other words,

*You cannot be a good lawyer if you have not read and studied other cases which are precedents to the case you have in hand.*

*You are a shallow Pharisee if you do not know about other cases concerning the issue you've raised.*

*You're a shallow Christian if you do not know the word of God concerning the issue you are dealing with or what you are going through right now.*

The Lord decided to give them a case study, based on King David, the man after God's heart, the great worshipper and psalmist of Israel.

## Case Study 1

Read Verse 3-5

The Pharisee could be saying:

"Wow, how did he know all about that?"

Two things: you could say he read it. Don't forget he was not happy that the Pharisees had not even read that portion of scripture.

Or you could also say, "Well, he was there when it happened." He is God. Before Abraham, He was. The **'I am'** that has always been and the Lord of all things.

He was there when David entered the house of God and took and ate the consecrated bread, which he was not even supposed to touch. It was meant only for the priests. Not only did he touch and eat it, he also gave some to his disciples to eat because he cared for them and was concerned that they would not faint with hunger.

In other words, the Lord was saying to the Pharisees: *So that you may know that I am the same God, the One who had compassion on David and his soldiers; I am the same God who will have compassion on my hungry disciples.*

Then comes verse 5 of our text, which must have hit the Pharisees like a ton of bricks. **"The Son of Man is Lord also of the Sabbath."**

He said in essence, *"You may or may not believe who I am; but I am God. Whatever else I am Lord of, I am Lord **also** of the Sabbath." The Son of Man owns the Sabbath; the Son of Man instituted the Sabbath and the Son of Man knows the purpose of the Sabbath. It is not for oppression and punishment but for compassion, rest and freedom.*

*The Sabbath is meant to bless you and do you good, not as a tool or means of oppression and doing evil. To watch people starve to death when there's food to feed them is not keeping the Sabbath."*

Let's go back to Deuteronomy 5:14-15 and ask: 'Why was the Sabbath set up and by whom?'

God told the Israelites, *"Six days you shall labour and do all your work but the seventh day is the Sabbath of the Lord."* The Sabbath is for man to rest because man gets tired and fatigued. God does not.

However, it is the Sabbath of the Lord and people need to take it seriously and take time off to rest. God made it a command so that man would take it seriously, hence the Sabbath of the Lord.

Look at verse 15 of Deuteronomy 5: Here the Lord was reminding them and correcting what was a huge misconception at that time, which is still a huge misconception today - that the Sabbath was meant for God. The Lord was saying:

"Don't forget why I'm doing this. When you were slaves in Egypt, you worked day and night for your slave masters. You suffered so much and had no rest. I rescued you from those who enslaved you, who would have loved to keep you as slaves forever. Now you are free. Don't keep working and treating yourselves like slaves. If anything, you are now my slaves. Take a day off and rest your body. It's my day, which I have given you. It is the day of the Lord, your master, but I am giving it to you and for you, for I am the Lord, your owner, your master; not the Egyptians.

Learn from me how masters should treat their servants. When you were in Egypt, they maltreated you and your household. They did all manners of evil to you.

*Now you are liberated*
*Now you are consecrated*
*Now you are redeemed*
*Now you are rescued*
*Divine military operation*
*Has won your salvation*
*You cannot be slaves again*
*Now you are born again*
*You are saved and free,*
*Completely and utterly free.*

Take one of my days off and rest. Give your household a break, including your guests and visitors.

Let your servants too have it as a day of rest. Your enemies heaped burdens on you to kill, to steal and to destroy you; to do all manner of evil against you. I have reversed the whole thing. You are no longer slaves to them. You don't work for man anymore, but for me. My plan is to give you life and give it to you more abundantly.

You are free and can rest whenever you can but I am giving you one day in the week specifically for rest – and to meditate on my goodness and how I have saved you. Mine is to do good not to do evil."

Praise the Lord!

So, in summary, we learn:

· That God set up the Sabbath as a day of rest from our works, our troubles and our burdens.
· That God is the Lord, the owner of the Sabbath. He owns seven days a week and has ordered us to take one off and rest.
· That there is a difference between our Father God and our former slave masters.

God knows our needs and he knows our frailty. He knows what the body is made of and knows we need to rest. Who would you like to obey - God or a slave master? Of course, there are a variety of other slave masters today, completely different from the ones the Israelites served.

Who is your slave master?

Is it your wife or your children?

Is it your husband or your bosses?

Is it your career or your business?

Is it your family or your community?

Is it your riches or your fame?

Don't forget that the Scripture says, *"to whom- soever you yield yourself servant to obey, the same is your master"* (Roman 6:16). Anything, whatever it is, that makes it impossible for you to have time to rest or fellowship with the Lord, that same thing has become your master. The Sabbath of the Lord is actually for you to rest, not for God to rest. He does not need the rest or meditation.

Praise the Lord!

### *Keeping the Sabbath:*

The laws that the Pharisees had about keeping the Sabbath were so harsh that it is hard to know where they got them from. They were so harsh, we don't know on which principles they based them on. They were no longer based on the compassion of the Lord of the Sabbath, but on the tormenting strategies of the devil. "There is food surplus and plenty but don't touch it. There's only 24 hours to go till the end of the Sabbath. That child, that woman, is boiling with fever. There's a doctor here with penicillin but don't go there. Let them suffer for only 24 hours more. We are keeping the Sabbath."

*The Lord Yeshua says, "That is not God."*

*The Lord Yeshua says, "That is not good."*

## Case Study 2

The first case study which the Lord Yeshua presented to them was from the Old Testament (King

David). A week later, again on the Sabbath day and in the Synagogue, the second case study presented itself to them. It was not two millennia away and far-fetched. No, it was right in front of them – sort of in their face.

Let's read it:

> [6]Now it happened on another Sabbath, also, that He entered the synagogue and taught. And a man was there whose right hand was withered. [7]So the scribes and Pharisees watched Him closely, whether He would heal on the Sabbath, that they might find an accusation against Him. [8]But he knew their thoughts, and said to the man who had the withered hand, "Arise and stand here." And he arose and stood. [9]Then Jesus said to them, "I will ask you one thing: Is it lawful on the Sabbath to do good or to do evil, to save life or to destroy?" [10]And when He had looked around at them all, He said to the man, "Stretch out your hand." And he did so, and his hand was restored as whole as the other. [11]But they were filled with rage, and discussed with one another what they might do to Jesus.

**(Luke 6:6-11)**

It is like the Lord Yeshua was saying to them, *"Hey listen, I was teaching on this issue of keeping the Sabbath last week. I don't think you fully understood it. I've come back again this week to teach a bit more on the subject. It is quite an evil thing that this man has been in such a state among you for such a long time and you couldn't do anything about it. Well, I am the Lord, the great Physician. I can do something for him. I can relieve him of the pain on his withered right hand. That would be a good thing, wouldn't it? I could leave him too; that would be evil, wouldn't it? What do you think? Which shall I do, good or evil? Go on, tell me."*

None of them could answer. Don't forget his first illustration was from the Old Testament, the second was a man right there in front of them. This man obviously was in pain. He had always been in pain. We don't know for how long he had been living with the pain of his withered hand.

The Scribes and the Pharisees were watching the Lord Yeshua closely. Would he or would he not? They were watching him closely, not to see the good he would do, but in order that they might find reason to accuse him. Do you know people like that today? Or are you like that yourself; never seeing the good in other people, always looking for evil and reasons to accuse them?

The Lord diverted the attention from his accusers and placed it on the good He was about to do to the man with the withered hand.

How do you defeat your problems? How do you defeat the enemy's onslaught on your life? Is it by worrying about it or by focusing all your attention on the attacks and on the problems? That is what the enemy would like you to do: to create anxiety, worry and fear.

The Lord shifted the emphasis from the Pharisees who were the problems to the man who needed help; he replaced the focus on evil with the focus on the good. We should borrow a leaf from that and learn from the Lord. Take your attention away from the problem and the power you're heaping on the devil. Go out and do some good and put the devil to shame.

Verse 8

**Rise up and come forward.** The Lord says to you as you read this: *"Get up from your downtrodden state. You've suffered for far too long. Now is the time for you to get up, not only from your state of poverty and shame, but I also say, 'Move forward and closer to me for your blessing'."*

How long have you stayed at the back? How long have you been downtrodden? The Lord is saying today is the day to come out from the shadows. Today is the day to come into your blessing and your riches. Today is the day you come into your rest. Today is your Sabbath day. Your God is the Lord of the Sabbath. Yeshua, the Messiah, your Friend, is the Lord of the Sabbath. You do not need to suffer any longer like slaves. You are no longer in Egypt if you put your trust in him. If you will rise up today and come closer to him, the Lord, your healer, the Great Physician, will deliver you from all your troubles.

### *Keeping the Sabbath*

At this juncture, the Lord has put the problem on the centre stage. Let us gaze at it, reason it out seriously and know what the problem actually is.

The Scripture says, "My people perish because of lack of knowledge." Maybe none of them even knew what the problem was. Maybe none of us today know what the problem or what the accusation is that the enemy has levelled against us and against our Lord. So here, the Lord Yeshua wanted to help them a little bit. He says, 'Come, let us reason together, because my people perish for lack of knowledge.'

The problem is...

What is your motive? Whatever it is that you want to do. Whatever it is that you are doing, what is your motive? To do good or to do harm? To save life or to destroy it? To let people stew in their suffering or to save them from hunger, pain and misery? Which one would it be for you? Even in keeping the Sabbath or keeping the ordinances of the Bible, what is your motive?

Today, many Christian churches keep their Sabbath rest on Sunday. Some say this is because the Lord rose from the dead on Sunday; that they had to change the Sabbath rest of the Lord, which was originally instituted for sunset on Friday to sunset on Saturday evening. Others also say that there was no need for the change. They state that the Lord never gave anyone (alive or dead) any instructions to change the Sabbath day of rest.

This group of apologists further state that when human beings do their own things without consulting God, adverse consequences always follow. They say that many Christians today are worshipping the

Sun god, since Sunday is said to be the day for the Sun god. They believe majority of "Christians" are idol worshippers who worship the Sun god and that the consequences of our disobedience are seen in the way the world is heading today. Their favourite Scripture is *"There is a way which seemeth right unto a man, but the end thereof are the ways of death"* (Proverbs 14:12).

Majority of church-goers today were born into going to church on Sundays. In church, they would also read out their Ten Commandments and one of them would say, "Remember the Sabbath day to keep it holy."

Irrespective of what day people choose to go to a place of worship, I am not sure whether there are any group of Christians who keep the Sabbath rest of the Lord the way it was intended. If this sounds like a wild statement, I apologise straightaway. On the other hand, I would like to know such Christians; when and what they actually do to keep the Sabbath rest of the Lord.

Even if you were born into or live in a culture and environment where going to regular Sunday services is your Sabbath rest, how do you observe that rest? It may not be the original day set up for the Sabbath, but do you have a day in the week when you take a break from your work to rest and meditate on the goodness of God?

I know many Christians who read this would say, 'that sounds like a good idea but when do I have time for a rest?"

I have a very strong belief that God who created us, knows everything about our fragile frame and knows that it would get weak within the course of the week's chores. He therefore commanded us to have a day to rest and rejuvenate our bodies. The actual day that people observe the "Sabbath" today may be completely different from the original day that was set up, but the point is not about the day but about man having a rest. The Sabbath was made for man and not man for the Sabbath (Mark2:27).

When you and I go to church on Sundays, the question is, what do we go to do? Do we go to worship God, to rest, or to show that we were present? What are your motives? Do we really get to rest or has Sunday become an even busier day in our lives? You may not even have Sunday available, let alone keep the Sabbath rest. You are probably working seven days a week! The Lord is saying for your own benefit, take a day to rest. You have only one body given to you by the Lord; look after it. If the job does not change you for God, change your job for God.

If you work on Sundays, what is your motive? If you do your business on Sundays or make Sunday your shopping day, what is your motive? Of course, you know that the issue is not whether it is Friday, Saturday or Sunday. But do you have a day off in the week? If yes, is it a day of rest or a day for shopping and washing? Is it for you a Sabbath rest of the Lord, giving thanks unto God for his goodness to you and to your family?

Are you with any of the Emergency Services? Is your Sunday work an emergency or is it more overtime? Is it necessary? Was it compulsory or did you choose it? Do you have a Sabbath rest with the Lord, irrespective of what day it is? If you are one of those who adhere strictly to the Sabbath day law, what is the motive behind your unbending strictness? Is it your love for the Lord or is it your own power control mechanism?

In the passage we read, the Pharisees could not give the Lord any answers. He looked around but no one was able to answer him. He gave them the benefit of the doubt and consulted them. If there was a reason why he should not have healed the man, they should have told him – after all, they were the teachers of the law. Of course, they could not find it anywhere in the law where it says not to heal anyone or do a good deed on the Sabbath. The Lord Yeshua knew all that. He is the Lord of the Sabbath.

Without faith it is impossible to please God. Everything we do in God and with God should be done in faith, in love and with compassion.

Imagine what would have happened if the man did not obey. If he did not get up and move forward, how could he have received from the Lord? I don't know what your lowly position is at the moment; the Lord is calling you to get up and come closer to him. Do it in faith, trust him and he will surely lift you up.

Let's look at verse 10: (*my paraphrase again*).

*"There is a problem to solve; is there anyone here able to start solving it? Is there anyone here who can help this poor man with the problem of a withered hand? Anyone? No? Going, going... gone!*

Turning to the man with a withered right hand, he says:

*Well, as you can see, there's no one here (or anywhere else) who can help you.*
*They are not healers. They may pretend that they are but the truth is, they're not. They are pretenders.*
*The truth is, I am the only one who can heal you. Stretch out your heart to me and be restored. Stretch out your hand to me and receive."*
*Stretch out your hand again today.*
*In the name of the Lord Yeshua, wherever you may be.*
*Be healed today.*

The question is, who are you stretching out your hands to? Who are you expecting to help or heal you? Are you looking at the Pope at the Holy See, your bishop or archbishops, your apostles, prophets, ministers or pastors? None of them can help you. Not even the best of us can.

We are not healers; we are only instruments. Only God can heal. Don't get me wrong, God is still in the business of healing people. He still uses his servants as instruments to heal. The servants always give the glory for the healing and the miracles back to God. They never overemphasise their part in the healing. They never make you lose focus on God, the Healer.

Read verse 11

Why do you think they were filled with rage? Was it because they hated the good he was doing? No. They were jealous because he was doing things that they were not able to do. They were fading away in popularity and losing respect. Afraid the people would abandon them and follow this "young upstart" (as they saw him), they were prepared to kill him in order to remain famous as public figures. His presence was a threat to them.

The question is: "What are you prepared to do in order to hold on to power? Whatever it is, is it of the Lord? It is one thing keeping the Sabbath and another thing keeping the Sabbath of the Lord, for the sake of the Lord.

Let Us Pray:
*Father God who made our glorious bodies*
*Till Adam's sin concocted these abodes*
*And left us with these fragile fickle frames.*
*Father God, your weekdays one to seven*
*You gave a day for us to rest and pray*
*I pray today that we will utilise*
*This gift of love that you have given us*
*In Yeshua's name – the Son of God indeed.*
*AMEN!*

# 4

# COUNTING THE COST
# OF DISCIPLESHIP

—⟨⟨⟨⟩⟩⟩—

Luke 6:12-29

Many of the things that the Lord Yeshua did as recorded in the Bible were not necessarily because He needed to do them for Himself, but because He wanted to use those opportunities to teach His followers down through the ages how to conduct their lives.

One of such opportunities is as recorded in verses 12-16 of Luke chapter 6.

Before Yeshua could choose his apostles out of the large number of disciples around Him, He had to find a quiet place, where He could pray and meditate on what He was about to do. Being God in human flesh, He did not have to do this; but He used it as an occasion to teach his followers to always consult God before making their choices and decisions.

He was going to take a big step and choose twelve out of the many disciples that were with Him. He was going to commission and send them forth for special duties of church planting, spreading the gospel and making more disciples for Him all over the world. Hence His need for a quiet time with God, away from the hustle and bustle of everyday life.

## The Twelve Apostles

[12] Now it came to pass in those days that He went out to the mountain to pray, and continued all night in prayer to God. [13] And when it was day, He called His disciples to Himself; and from them He chose twelve whom He also named apostles: [14] Simon, whom He also named Peter, and Andrew his brother; James and John; Philip and Bartholomew; [15] Matthew and Thomas; James the son of Alphaeus, and Simon called the Zealot; [16] Judas the son of James, and Judas Iscariot who also became a traitor.

**(Luke 6:12–16)**

Here is how you can remember the names of the twelve apostles;

*There were two Simons:*
*one called Peter and the other called the Zealot.*
*There were two Jameses;*
*One, the son of Zebedee and brother of John, the other the son of Alpheus, also known as James the Younger.*
*There were also two Judases;*

*One called Judas or Thaddeus, the son of James
and the other Judas Iscariot, who betrayed Him.*

*Then there were Andrew, the brother of Simon
Peter and John the beloved, the brother of James;
Thomas, the doubter and Matthew or Levi, the former
tax collector.*

*There was also Philip and his friend Bartholomew
– also known as Nathaniel Bartholomew, 'an Israel-
ite indeed in whom is no guile.' (John 1:47).*

The twelve were from all sorts of backgrounds,
but of note is the fact that there were two sets of fishermen brothers; Simon Peter and his brother Andrew,
plus James and his brother John, the sons of Zebedee.
These were the brothers who He used the metaphor
of their trade to say that He was going to make them
fishers of men rather than fishers of fish.

[5]These twelve Jesus sent out after instructing
them: "Do not go in the way of the Gentiles,
and do not enter any city of the Samaritans;
[6]but rather go to the lost sheep of the house of
Israel. [7]And as you go, preach, saying, 'The
kingdom of heaven is at hand.' [8]Heal the
sick, raise the dead, cleanse the lepers, cast
out demons. Freely you received, freely give.
[9]Do not acquire gold, or silver, or copper for
your money belts, [10]or a bag for your journey,
or even two coats, or sandals, or a staff; for
the worker is worthy of is support. [11]And
whatever city or village you enter, inquire

who is worthy in it, and stay at his house until you leave that city.

[12]As you enter the house, give it your greeting. [13]If the house is worthy, give it your blessing of peace. But if it is not worthy, take back your blessing of peace. [14]Whoever does not receive you, nor heed your words, as you go out of that house or that city, shake the dust off your feet. [15]Truly I say to you, it will be more tolerable for the land of Sodom and Gomorrah in the day of judgment than for that city.

[16]"Behold, I send you out as sheep in the midst of wolves; so be shrewd as serpents and innocent as doves. [17]But beware of men, for they will hand you over to the courts and scourge you in their synagogues; [18]and you will even be brought before governors and kings for My sake, as a testimony to them and to the Gentiles. [19]But when they hand you over, do not worry about how or what you are to say; for it will be given you in that hour what you are to say. [20]For it is not you who speak, but it is the Spirit of your Father who speaks in you.

[21]"Brother will betray brother to death, and a father his child; and children will rise up against parents and cause them to be put to death. [22]You will be hated by all because of

My name, but it is the one who has endured to the end who will be saved. [23]"But whenever they persecute you in one city, flee to the next; for truly I say to you, you will not finish going through the cities of Israel until the Son of Man comes.

## (Matthew 10:5-23)

Verses 17-18

These verses may look simple but they are loaded with symbols and meaning. First, we have established that the Lord considered it important that He went to the mountain to pray before the big task of choosing His twelve apostles. Secondly, verse 17 says 'he descended with them, and stood on a level plane...' He stood on the same level with them, thus showing humility and solidarity with his disciples.

In those days, it was a usual practice for teachers or mentors to stand or sit on a higher plane than where his students are seated. This was done so that there would be no mistaking who the teacher was. It was also done so the teacher could stand out from the crowd and be seen by everyone who wishes to hear him without distraction or obstruction by other bodies.

In this passage, the Lord showed His humility by coming down and standing on the same level with His disciples and everyone else. Through this act, he was teaching us to put ourselves on the same level as our brothers and sisters, especially those who we are trying to help. We must humble ourselves and put ourselves in the shoes of the 'great throng of people' who will come from far and near to hear us and be healed of whatsoever it may be that is troubling them (Verse 18).

In a nutshell, Yeshua demonstrated to His disciples that nothing should be done through strife or vainglory, but in lowliness of heart, everyone should esteem others better than themselves. He humbled Himself and taught us that humility is part of the cost of discipleship.

This same attitude can be seen in what He said to His disciples in Mark 10:42-45:

> [42]Calling them to Himself, Jesus said to them, "You know that those who are recognized as rulers of the Gentiles lord it over them; and their great men exercise authority over them. [43]But it is not this way among you, but whoever wishes to become great among you shall be your servant; [44]and whoever wishes to be first among you shall be slave of all. [45]For even the Son of Man did not come to be served, but to serve, and to give His life a ransom for many."

**(Mark 10:42-45)**

Verse 19

Everyone was trying to touch Yeshua in order to receive virtue – the power to heal and restore – that was coming out from Him. Being the centre of attraction and attention can be such a big temptation that could easily make people lose their focus and become haughty. But the Lord Yeshua was not like that. He was the epitome of humility and He taught His lessons using Himself as an example.

Verse 20

From this verse onwards, we see the Lord doing what He always did so beautifully throughout His ministry as a master Teacher. The crowd would gather; He would speak in the earshot of everyone in the vicinity, but He would direct His teaching at a specific group of people – be it the Scribes, Lawyers, Pharisees or his disciples. Here, everyone was listening, but He was teaching His disciples what to expect as they counted the cost of discipleship. In this way, everyone heard and everyone learned the lessons, even if the specific teachings were for a different group of people.

## THE BEATITUDES

Verse 20

He said to them: Blessed are the poor (in spirit, Matt 5:3), for theirs is the kingdom of God.

First of all, the word blessed has sacredness about it. It is a word that has always had its origin as something emanating from God; favour or goodwill that He bestows upon those of whom He speaks well. These favours and goodwill, of course, are not without their benefits.

To be blessed by God automatically implies that the person so blessed has or will receive the good benefits or reward that go with the blessing. While blessings produce joy, happiness and fulfilment, woes produce the opposite effect. Woes or curses are wishes or pronouncements that the recipient receives evil or calamity of the worst kind.

Verse 20, however, is talking about being 'poor in spirit,' which continues the theme of humility that the Lord was addressing in verse 19. To be 'poor in spirit' is to realise how poor or bankrupt one is with regards to the spiritual food of the word of God. We are being taught here to see ourselves as poor and humble, always in need of spiritual nourishment. This will turn our hearts towards the only place it can be found, which is the Kingdom of God.

Verse 21

Blessed are you who hunger now, for you shall be satisfied. Blessed are you who weep now, for you shall laugh.

Whatever it is that you hunger for **now**; whether it is spiritual or physical food, you shall be satisfied. Whatever it is that is making you weep **now,** you shall have the last laugh over it later. You will emerge the winner in the end.

We must not overlook the keyword **now** in these two sentences. 'Now' is in the present, indicating prevailing hunger and weeping periods. But these two sentences imply that the hunger and weeping will not overwhelm us on the long run; they will not last forever. This also assures that our lives will be spared and preserved until the period when we shall receive our blessings, be satisfied, and laugh again.

These are God's promises. They cannot fail. We need to hang unto them whenever we find ourselves in difficult and trying circumstances. Hence, 'comfort one another with these words.'

Verses 22–23

In counting the cost of discipleship, the Lord warns His disciples not to give up because of mistreatment. He lets them know that time will come when men will hate them, ostracise them, insult them and even tell all manner of lies against them because of Him. (Do you find this hard to believe? It happened just as He said it would, especially during the persecution of Christians in Rome. Persecutions and false accusation of Christians are still happening today all around the world). The Lord says they should be glad and leap for joy because as blessed people who have found favour with God, they would have great rewards in heaven.

Moreover, they should be encouraged to know that they were not the first and may not be the last to receive mistreatment and evil machinations from evil doers. He wanted them to be ready, to arm themselves with the facts and to know that what they will encounter had happened before to their predecessors.

Verses 24-26

These verses teach us that in counting the cost of discipleship, the thing that should help us decide where to pitch our tent of allegiance is the end of the journey, not the **now** or the beginning. We are made to understand that the table will be turned in the end, against all sinners and perpetrators of evil. Those who are rich **now** and have no care in the world will be bankrupt then; they will have no blessings or favour of God. They will not have a part in the Kingdom of God.

Those who are well fed now will go hungry. Those who are laughing and enjoying themselves now at the expense of other people, will regret living that kind of lifestyle. They will have longer torment in the eternity of hell than the short period of enjoyment they had here on earth.

In counting the cost of discipleship, the disciples were to learn right from the onset that they were not going to be lying down on beds of roses; that they were not going to be in the 'good-book' of everyone. As a matter of fact, as a disciple, if you find yourself in the good-book of everyone, you should go back and re-examine what your life has been depicting. If everyone is comfortable and no one is ever touched by what you are saying, perhaps you need to wash your mouth with the soup and water of the word of God and start again.

Here, the Lord warns His disciples not to be deceived by the applause and adulations of the people. 'If they keep speaking well of you, they will get under your skin. If they do, you will lose focus; you will end up compromised and will become too careful with what you say. You may even begin to dilute the truth to suit and sooth your hearers. In the end, you will have nothing to show for all the running around, preaching and hard work that you had done. You will end up with lamentations of woe. Brothers and sisters, this will not be your portion in Yeshua's name. Amen.

Verses 27-29

It has been established from the verses before these that persecutions will come. Believers will be maltreated and ill-treated. But in these three verses the Lord took His teaching on to a higher, tougher notch than what had ever been heard before. Naturally, in normal circumstances, when someone declares himself your enemy, you are supposed to hate them because they do not wish you well.

When someone curses you, you are supposed to curse him back, even if you have to cover your mouth or curse him under your breath. When someone hits you on the cheek, in normal circumstances, you will at least try to defend yourself. But to present them with the other cheek on a platter of gold, saying, 'Hit me, hit me, hit me!' You can imagine how this new way of looking at things may have shocked the Jews who had been waiting for a leader, a conquering messiah, who would lead them into a march for sweet revenge against the Romans. It would not sit well with them. However, that is what the Master 'ordered' for those who would be His disciples even unto this generation.

We all know that love is sweet. In fact love, or to be loved, is the most beautiful thing in the whole of existence. Here we see the Lord teaching that the most beautiful thing in the world, which is love, can be used as a weapon against evil.

Because of love for people and their souls, if someone is your enemy and hates you, show him love. If someone curses you and wishes you calamities of the worst kind and even hits you, the Lord says, love them, wish them well and pray for them. You are not to have a retaliatory or revengeful character. They may even take away your property, your sustenance and your dignity; still love and care for them because you might be the instrument by which God will bring them from the kingdom of darkness into His kingdom of light. You are unique. You are not like them. Do not act like an unbeliever. Remember when the time comes to obey your Master.

It is important to state here that as human beings, verses 27–29 goes against the grain of our natural way of thinking or doing things. It is not easy to grasp or understand. As a matter of fact, it is easier said than done. Honestly speaking, it will not be easy to follow; it will be difficult to do. However, as we can see, they are the Lord Yeshua's instructions to His disciples. He knows that we cannot manage them on our own. All we need to do as we count the cost of discipleship, is learn and know what the instructions are and ask Him to help us do them when the time comes.

Luke 6:30-49

[30]Give to everyone who asks of you. And from him who takes away your goods do not

ask them back. [31]And just as you want men to do to you, you also do to them likewise.

[32]"But if you love those who love you, what credit is that to you? For even sinners love those who love them. [33]And if you do good to those who do good to you, what credit is that to you? For even sinners do the same. [34]And if you lend to those from whom you hope to receive back, what credit is that to you? For even sinners lend to sinners to receive as much back. [35]But love your enemies, do good, and lend, hoping for nothing in return; and your reward will be great, and you will be sons of the Most High. For He is kind to the unthankful and evil. [36]Therefore be merciful, just as your Father also is merciful.

[37]"Judge not, and you shall not be judged. Condemn not, and you shall not be condemned. Forgive, and you will be forgiven. [38]Give, and it will be given to you: good measure, pressed down, shaken together, and running over will be put into your bosom. For with the same measure that you use, it will be measured back to you."
[39]And He spoke a parable to them: "Can the blind lead the blind? Will they not both fall into the ditch? [40]A disciple is not above his teacher, but everyone who is perfectly trained will be like his teacher. [41]And why do you look at the speck in your brother's eye, but do

not perceive the plank in your own eye? [42]Or how can you say to your brother, 'Brother, let me remove the speck that is in your eye,' when you yourself do not see the plank that is in your own eye? Hypocrite! First remove the plank from your own eye, and then you will see clearly to remove the speck that is in your brother's eye.

[43]"For a good tree does not bear bad fruit, nor does a bad tree bear good fruit. [44]For every tree is known by its own fruit. For men do not gather figs from thorns, nor do they gather grapes from a bramble bush. [45]A good man out of the good treasure of his heart brings forth good; and an evil man out of the evil treasure of his heart brings forth evil. For out of the abundance of the heart his mouth speaks.

[46]"But why do you call Me 'Lord, Lord,' and not do the things which I say? [47]Whoever comes to Me, and hears My sayings and does them, I will show you whom he is like: [48]He is like a man building a house, who dug deep and laid the foundation on the rock. And when the flood arose, the stream beat vehemently against that house, and could not shake it, for it was founded on the rock. [49]But he who heard and did nothing is like a man who built a house on the earth without a foundation, against which the stream beat

vehemently; and immediately it fell. And the ruin of that house was great."

**(Luke 6:30-49)**

Verse 30 says:

'Give to everyone who asks of you....'

This verse implies that as a child of God you will always have enough to spare. The statement did not say 'give to everyone who asks you if you have it or can afford it.' By implication, this instruction is saying that you will always have it, so do not deny the people in need who will ask of you. It is so clear in that verse that God was sure of Himself. He had faith in Himself, knowing that He was Yahweh Jireh, our Provider. He is asking us to have faith in Him. He is asking of us to be the conduit with which He distributes His goodness and love throughout the world, even unto those who have declared God their enemy.

## THE GOLDEN RULE

Verse 31

This verse is what is known as the golden rule. **'Just as you want people to treat you, treat them in the same way.' (NASB)** Matthew 7:12 renders the same statement like this: '**Therefore, however you want people to treat you, so treat them, for this is the Law and the Prophets.**' Besides John 3:16, these verses depicting the golden rule must rank among the most important as well as the most popular verses in the Bible.

Similar verses are found in the Old Testament, in Leviticus 19:18 and 34. It is either the Lord Yeshua was quoting from the Old Testament and perfecting an Old Testament saying, or that these verses were brand new from Him, especially where it says: '**for this is the Law and the Prophets.**' In other words, loving our neighbours as ourselves because we love God or because of the love God, is the sum total of what our whole existence, including our preaching, teaching, prophesying or even the written down scriptures, is all about.

Verses 32–36

Loving those who love us may come easy but loving an enemy is one of the hardest things anyone can be asked to do. Theses verses admonish the disciples to go the extra mile. It is asking the disciples to do acts that are unique and different from what the ordinary man on the street would do.

What was required of the disciples - to love and do good to their enemies – is definitely a difficult thing to ask. The disciples were to persevere and in doing those acts because that was what set them apart from sinners and the rest of the world. Sinners love those who love them and have no such compunction to love their enemies. But the disciples are to love their enemies because they have a duty to obey their Master, whose characteristic is love for everyone.

Verse 37

"Do not judge, and you will not be judged; and do not condemn, and you will not be condemned; pardon, and you will be pardoned.

We must be careful not to take the above verse to mean that the Lord was asking his disciples to do away with their ability to discern between good and evil or between right and wrong. He certainly did not mean for them to bury their heads in the sand – 'hearing no evil, seeing no evil.'

On the contrary, he was warning them not to be like the Scribes and the Pharisees who had the habit of judging other people harshly by heaping burdens and punishment on them, whilst they 'themselves will not move them (**the burdens**) with one of their fingers' (Matthew 23:4).

Verses 37-38 are more or less saying the same thing. What you put in is what you take out; in terms of your judgement, your love and your mercy or the lack of them. The Lord says: give, give and keep giving of your love and of yourself, you will never out-give God. Whatever you give, He will definitely use other people or other circumstances to overwhelm you with His blessings.

Verses 39-40

The ultimate end of discipleship, as far as the Lord was concerned, was taking the mantle of leadership from the Master. It also meant leading a lot of people who are blind spiritually. If they were going to be leading the blind, at least they should be different; they should at least be enlightened and full of light. Otherwise, they would lead other people astray and they would all fall into the ditch of errors.

To be a leader of other people, a master with disciples, one has to have that extra edge, that extra knowledge, that extra strength or discipline that the disciples would crave to acquire. No disciple goes to serve a master unless they believe they would be better off, enriched in the end than they were before submitting to such a master. No servant or student goes to a master unless he or she believes they would learn some new things to improve their lives. Disciples learn, build on and establish their worldview on the strength of the teachings of their masters.

In these two verses, the Lord was admonishing His disciples to diligently learn from Him in all manner of humility and perfection if they were going to be His disciples. They needed to study to be full of the knowledge of their Master who also was their source of enlightenment. If they were untrained and empty-headed, they would also produce untrained and empty-headed disciples who would not amount to anything or affect any changes in the world. Because, He said, everyone that is perfect shall surely be perfect after his own master.

Verses 41-42

The Lord admonished his disciples to first do a thorough self-examination before embarking on the crusade to rid society of all that was wrong with it. It would be a great shame, He says, if they started pointing accusing fingers on others, even for minor offences, while huge 'skeletons' were being pulled out from their own cupboards. They were to be empathetic, tolerant, kind and forgiving of others as they too would like to be forgiven.

Verses 43–45

In counting the cost of discipleship, one must not be a pretender (verse 42). You must be genuine and not hypocritical. You cannot pretend to be who you are not. Even pretenders and deceivers will not be able to pretend or deceive people for ever; neither can they deceive God at all.

What one sows is what one reaps. Spiritual seed will always bear spiritual fruit and good works. Sinful seed and its activities will always bear evil fruits and evil results. No matter how long one pretends, what is on the inside will always come out on the outside for the whole world to see. "For good trees do not produce bad fruit or bad trees produce good fruit" (verse 43). It is by your fruit that people will know you and of whose disciple you are.

In this segment, it is like the Lord Yeshua was saying to His disciples:

*I have called you and you have come*
*I know you want to be my disciples*

*You must understand the seriousness*
*of your calling as you count the cost.*
*God is good, all the time*
*I am God and I am your Master*
*Everything you do must resemble Me*
*Everything you do must represent Me*
*You must serve me with all your heart*
*From what you know of Me.*

*"For a good man out of the good treasure of his heart brings forth good; and an evil man out of the evil treasure of his heart brings forth evil. For out of the abundance of the heart his mouth speaks."*

Verses 46-47

In these two verses above, it sounds like the Lord was asking His disciples a rhetorical question.

*"What's the point? What's the point in calling me Lord, Lord and not willing to do my biddings? You need to understand what you are getting yourself into. If you are going to be my disciple, I need to be your Lord. I need to own you completely – spirit, soul and body."*

There are only three main steps to true discipleship. First of all, you come to me. I call you, you come to me.

Secondly, you hear the words of my teachings. Thirdly, you go away and put into practice what I have instructed you to do, in order to achieve results. Coming to me is not enough. Just like becoming a Christian or being born-again is not enough. You need to learn the word of God. You need to learn the instructions. You need to "study to show yourself approved of God, a workman who does not need to be ashamed, rightly dividing the word of truth," as the Master would have been. Finally and thirdly, you go and do; you go and put into action what I have instructed you to do. Without these three components together we would still be lacking in our wanting to be the disciple of the Lord.

Verses 48–49

Being a disciple of the Lord requires careful study and calculation. Just like a builder, one has to research, survey and calculate thoroughly what kind of soil one would like to build upon – whether on sinking sand or the foundation of a solid rock. If they chose Him and did what He asked them to do, they will never go wrong. They will succeed and never fail. The Lord's admonition was good enough for the apostles and the early disciples. Look where it got them. The same admonition has been alive and dynamic. It is still relevant to us today as Christians. We too must count the cost of discipleship.

# LUKE CHAPTER 7

—∾—

# 5

# JUST SEND THE WORD

Luke 7:1-10

¹Now when he had ended all his sayings in the audience of the people, he entered into Capernaum. ²And a certain centurion's servant, who was dear unto him, was sick, and ready to die. ³And when he heard of Jesus, he sent unto him the elders of the Jews, beseeching him that he would come and heal his servant. ⁴And when they came to Jesus, they besought him instantly, saying, That he was worthy for whom he should do this: ⁵For he loveth our nation, and he hath built us a synagogue.

⁶Then Jesus went with them. And when he was now not far from the house, the centurion sent friends to him, saying unto him, Lord, trouble not thyself: for I am not worthy that thou shouldest enter under my roof: ⁷Wherefore neither thought I myself worthy to come unto thee: but say in a word, and my servant

shall be healed. [8]For I also am a man set under authority, having under me soldiers, and I say unto one, Go, and he goeth; and to another, Come, and he cometh; and to my servant, Do this, and he doeth it.

[9]When Jesus heard these things, he marvelled at him, and turned him about, and said unto the people that followed him, I say unto you, I have not found so great faith, no, not in Israel. [10]And they that were sent, returning to the house, found the servant whole that had been sick.

**(Luke 71-10)**

The word of God is for everyone - big or small, young or old. Previously in chapter 6, we see the Lord teaching his disciples on counting the cost of discipleship. He was teaching them in a public place. He directed his speech to them but he was speaking in the hearing of everyone present -whether they were male, female, young or old, in that vicinity, He was speaking to them all.

The same goes for us today. Someone might say, 'Well, that was for the disciples, not for me'. You might even say, *"Well, that was for the church leaders – bishops, pastors, elders and those church workers - certainly not me. I just breeze in and out of the church. I don't really want to get involved."* The Lord knew their minds and thought processes. He knows yours too. He is aware of what you are thinking and what you're going through.

In the story above, you must remember that the Lord Yeshua was standing there, dishing out his words in the hearing of all the people (all those that would hear him). Then came that crucial moment for him to demonstrate the ability and the power of the Word of God to go and do things, even without the Lord being physically present. He does not have to be physically visible before you can speak to him or before he can tackle your situation. All you need to do is send the word out to him and he will send the word out to deal with your issue.

Read the passage again (Luke 7:1-10).

The Lord did not just deal with the Jews. He did not just heal the rich and famous. He did not just save the citizens and the well-to-do. He was healing and restoring many to God. He came to heal and to save both the Jews and the Gentiles, including the young and the old, the slaves as well as their masters.

Verse 1

In this story, we know that the centurion was not a Jew. He was not one of the chosen people designated for Abrahamic blessings. He was a Roman citizen; the oppressors of the Jews. In other words, he was a big colonial master; an outcast and a bad person in the eyes of the Jews. Though this man was a *big man* and an enemy (per se), he had great qualities that the people admired.

He loved the Jewish nation and built their synagogues. Knowing what the Jews thought about them as foreign oppressors, this centurion did not think that he stood a chance as far as receiving any favours from the Lord Yeshua was concerned. He had to ask the elders to speak for him and to plead on his behalf as an outsider; thinking, *"There's no way He's going to turn around and look in my direction and if he does, he'll only see an outsider; a sinner full of iniquities."*

Aren't we all like this centurion sometimes in our mindset, even as redeemed, saved children of God?

Sometimes we think there's no way God is going to be interested in us or our problems. He's got more problems to sort out than to waste precious time on us sinners. We feel he has more important and more holy people to deal with and would not spare a moment with us.

This story demonstrates that the Lord Yeshua did not come only for the Jews. He did not come only for the centurion, the politicians, the top religious people or the celebrities of this world. He also came for the poor slaves that were nothing. He came for *you*.

In verse 2, we see that the Lord healed and saved the centurion's *slave* from Satan's destruction. It was not the centurion or the Jewish elders who needed help, but a foreign slave. In the same passage, we see the indication that in those days, slaves received favour or disfavour according to the wish of their master. They could not approach the Lord Yeshua for themselves or on their own behalf. If their master did not regard them much, then they received no favours, no attention, no healing and perhaps no deliverance from their problems. They might even die in them and that would be the end of it.

Praise God! Aren't you glad that you now belong to God and not to any man and that you're highly regarded by your master, the Lord Yeshua, the Messiah? All you have to do is send the word out to him and your situation will be dealt with. Because you are highly precious to him, you don't need to go through a middle man. You don't need to consult the bishops, the elders, the saints dead or alive; not even the angels or anyone else to get the Lord's attention regarding your situation. *Just send the Word!*

You need to know the power and authority that is in the Word before you can *send the Word.* You also need to understand who you are to Him and how he regards you before you can *send the Word!*

Two things:

· You can either realise that you are a hopeless, helpless sinner and no one (dead or alive) can help you, except the Lord Yeshua the Messiah, or
· You realise who you are as a son or daughter of God; the God who will never leave nor forsake you, who says he has come that you may have life and have it more abundantly.

Whichever of these two is the case, *just send the Word!*

These are the key criteria to receive from God - not how much you love the planet, the people, the animals or whether you are a philanthropist who has built this or that for the people. The Lord was not moved by those good deeds, neither did he comment on them.

Don't get me wrong; the Lord does not shun or disregard philanthropists. However, the third input criterion in the list below is the one he commented on.

Try these three steps yourself if you haven't done so before.

1. First, acknowledge that you are a sinner who does not stand a chance with God unless you repent of your sins.

2. Second, if you are a believer already, realise who you are in God and have faith in God's ability to save, deliver and provide for you at all times.

The third is in verses 6-10. You can read it again.

3. Whether you are a slave or a free man or woman, boy or girl; this is the one thing that God delights in, the one that makes Him glad – humility.

The Lord went everywhere: to the house of the poor, the house of the rich (the saint, the sinner), beside the sea-side, upon the hill top, in the wilderness, as well as in the city. Out of humility, this centurion man genuinely believed that his Roman mansion was not good enough and holy enough for the Lord to come into. What did he do? He just sent the word out and asked the Lord Yeshua to '***just send the word out'*** *too to heal his sick slave rather than bother coming into his house.*

Genuine humility will get you anywhere, especially the centre of God's heart. *Just send the Word* in humility.

There's power and authority in the Word. Just send the Word and you will see that though there is no telephone to heaven, the Lord who is your Master hears the faintest groaning of your heart. Just as in verse 10, his words travelled fast and distance was no barrier to him. As it was then, even so it is today.

## 6

# I AM THE
# RESURRECTION
# AND THE LIFE

—◦◦◦—

Luke 7:11-17

Sometime ago, in one of our Sunday services, we were blessed with a message from the Lord saying, *"Revival: there's still hope for you."* In this section, we will be looking at a similar word that means exactly the same thing. That word is *Resurrection.* We will be looking at Jesus' words, "I am the Resurrection and the Life."

Again, just like revival, to say that something or someone has resurrected implies that such a person or object was dead or lifeless but has now revived or come back to life.

Let's have a look at some Scriptures: Luke 7:11-17 and John 11:23-26.

> [11]Now it happened, the day after, that He went into a city called Nain; and many of His disciples went with Him, and a large crowd.

[12]And when He came near the gate of the city, behold, a dead man was being carried out, the only son of his mother; and she was a widow. And a large crowd from the city was with her. [13]When the Lord saw her, He had compassion on her and said to her, "Do not weep." [14]Then He came and touched the open coffin, and those who carried him stood still. And He said, "Young man, I say to you, arise." [15]So he who was dead sat up and began to speak. And He presented him to his mother. [16]Then fear came upon all, and they glorified God, saying, "A great prophet has risen up among us"; and, "God has visited His people." [17]And this report about Him went throughout all Judea and all the surrounding region.

### (Luke 7:11-17)

[23]Jesus said to her, "Your brother will rise again." [24]Martha said to Him, "I know that he will rise again in the resurrection at the last day." [25]Jesus said to her, "I am the resurrection and the life. He who believes in Me, though he may die, he shall live. [26]And whoever lives and believes in Me shall never die. Do you believe this?"

### (John 11:23-26)

"I am the resurrection and the life." This is the claim of our Master, the Lord Yeshua. No one else, either dead or alive, has ever made such a claim. When he said 'I am the resurrection,' it meant that He had the ability to bring things or people to life, even if they were dead. If they were dead or dying he is able to revive them and bring them back to life.

He said, "I am *the* resurrection and *the* life," not *a* resurrection and *a* life. In other words: "If you want to resurrect here and in the next life, you need only me. Without me, whether here on earth or in the here-after, you will not resurrect or have life."

He demonstrated this by the way he raised Lazarus from the dead, after being dead and buried for four days. He also demonstrated this by this account in Luke 7:11 where he raised back to life the son of the widow of Nain.

Finally he demonstrated what he says here by the way he rose from the grave and from the dead and continues to lead his children even till this day.

*I am the Resurrection and the Life.*

Let's go back to our text and see some of the characteristics of the Lord Yeshua, the Resurrection and the Life.


Verse 11

In this passage, we see a great crowd following him around wherever he went. He was a celebrity, if ever there was one. Everything he did or said was miraculous. People came in their droves to see and to hear him. But one of the things he did quite often was to go wherever there was great need. On this occasion the Spirit moved him to go to Nain. As he entered the gate, he found the community mourning. There was a widow who had only one son. This son had died and there was weeping and wailing by the community as they proceeded on their way to bury him.

Verse 12
The Lord Yeshua met them at the gate.

The gate is quite significant in both this story and in all our lives. It is through the gate of your soul that you can let in or throw away things that could make you dead or alive to God. In this story, they were going outside the gate. That is a place of hopelessness and vulnerability where everything dead is thrown away or buried in order not to contaminate the living within the gates.

Consider this woman. She was a widow. When her husband died, the woman must have heaped on this only son her future, her hopes, her dreams and her happiness. Can you imagine then how she felt when her only hope died? She was helpless *as well as* hopeless. She had the crowd of mourners but that was all they were: mourners. They had no power to help her. Majority of them might even be physically standing with her but only 'outside the gate,' and therefore unable to help her.

They cried and wailed and sympathised with her, but that was all they could do. As far as resurrection and life was concerned, they were useless. Then came in the Lord Yeshua, the Resurrection and the Life.

Verse 13
The Lord is full of love and compassion. He says to the woman and to the mourners – "Weep not." My

brothers and my sisters, the Lord Yeshua has compassion for you. He is ready to wipe away your tears. He is your Lord and your saviour and he says,

> "Weep Not, for I am the Resurrection and the Life. The devil has come to kill, to steal and to destroy, even from poor widows but I have come to give life and to give life more abundantly because 'I am the Resurrection and the Life.'"

> Dear friend, He is your comforter and he says to you "Weep Not."

Verse 14

There are some points to note here. The Lord Yeshua touched the coffin. He touched the dead. He raised the body and gave him back to his mother alive.

Remember:
1. Dead bodies were carried out outside the city gate. The reason was that dead bodies were classed as unclean. The community that lived within the gates, particularly the religious leaders, were not supposed to touch dead bodies because they would become contaminated. In other words, it would make them unclean.
2. The Lord Yeshua was a Rabbi; he knew the law. He knew also that contamination or defilement eventually could lead to death.

3. But the Lord is the Resurrection and the Life; the giver and taker-away of life. His touch brings new life to those he touches, because he himself is revival, resurrection and life.

Do you want revival in your life and in all that you do? Then allow the Lord Yeshua to touch you. He will touch all areas of your life that the world is not able to satisfy. He will give you peace and prosperity in a measure that you can never ever imagine.

At the back of everyone's mind is this nagging thought: "If we could just conquer death;" but the Lord Yeshua *already* conquered death! He has power over life and death.

That woman's case was hopeless until she met the Lord. Her son's case was hopeless until the Lord touched him. Your life is useless and your future, hopeless without Him.

Read verse 15

So he who was dead sat up and began to speak. And He presented him to his mother.

### (Luke 7:15)

Whenever the Lord Yeshua is on the scene, he makes people do the impossible. He makes you do things you were never able to do. The young man was no longer able to move his limbs. He was never going to speak again - he was dead! Then the Lord came into his life and made him to sit up. He also started to speak, which was a sign of life. If he sat up but never spoke, people would still be wondering whether he was alive or dead.

Have you been lying down dead? Have you been just a body without life? Has the Lord Yeshua touched you? Right now he's asking you to sit up. He's asking you to get up and be alive; to start speaking about Him that God may be glorified. He's calling you to wake up and stop being dead or playing dead. Being alive rather than dead is far more active and sweeter.

Verses 16-17

Notice that the Lord Yeshua did not announce in advance that he was going to perform miracles that evening. Our present-day preachers would announce, *"Tomorrow evening is going to be Miracle Service Night. Go home tonight and bring all your friends: the blind, the cripple or the lame. Tomorrow they will be healed."*

These people keep a date when they would perform miracles, but the Lord performed them every day as he sees the people and had compassion on them – whether it was one person or at a crowded meeting. He came to teach but miracles always followed him.

Even today, he is always performing great miracles in people's lives—every time and everywhere all over the world—bringing dead situations back to life. Indeed, he said, "I am the Resurrection and the Life."

# 7

# BE PATIENT
# WITH GOD

—⁓⁓—

Luke 7:18-35

Many people in the world today are impatient with God. They would even like to dictate to God how and when they want him (God) to perform this or that for them. Time and time again, we hear God saying in no uncertain words, like in the prophecy of Isaiah:

> [8]For my thoughts are not your thoughts, neither are your ways my ways, saith the LORD. [9]For as the heavens are higher than the earth, so are my ways higher than your ways, and my thoughts than your thoughts. [10]For as the rain cometh down, and the snow from heaven, and returneth not thither, but watereth the earth, and maketh it bring forth and bud, that it may give seed to the sower, and bread to the eater: [11]So shall my

word be that goeth forth out of my mouth:
it shall not return unto me void, but it shall
accomplish that which I please, and it shall
prosper in the thing whereto I sent it.

**(Isaiah 55:8-11)**

People want to tell God what to do and when
to do it.

When that does not happen as and when we
want it, we get angry and impatient with God.

If God takes every instruction of ours and does
everything how and when we want it, then He
would not be God. We would be; and He would
just be taking instructions and orders from us.

That is why in this section, the Lord really
wants us to learn to be patient and to ask ourselves
this probing and serious question: **What are you
looking for?**

Many times, people become angry and impatient with others but most especially with God
because they cannot see what they were looking
for. Being human, we think in human terms. But
God is spirit and he sees beyond our scope. He sees
the good, the better and the best. God is spirit and
they that worship Him must worship him in spirit
and in truth. However, when we are weighed down
by the flesh, we lose the strength of the spirit. We
also lose the truth of who God is and the truth of
the real motive of our desires and requests. Today,
God's message is:

**Whatever you are looking for, be patient with God.**

Let's read our text:

[18]And the disciples of John shewed him of all these things. [19]And John calling unto him two of his disciples sent them to Jesus, saying, Art thou he that should come? or look we for another? [20]When the men were come unto him, they said, John Baptist hath sent us unto thee, saying, Art thou he that should come? or look we for another? [21]And in that same hour he cured many of their infirmities and plagues, and of evil spirits; and unto many that were blind he gave sight.

[22]Then Jesus answering said unto them, Go your way, and tell John what things ye have seen and heard; how that the blind see, the lame walk, the lepers are cleansed, the deaf hear, the dead are raised, to the poor the gospel is preached. [23]And blessed is he, whosoever shall not be offended in me. [24]And when the messengers of John were departed, he began to speak unto the people concerning John, What went ye out into the wilderness for to see? A reed shaken with the wind? [25]But what went ye out for to see? A man clothed in soft raiment? Behold, they which are gorgeously apparelled, and live delicately, are in kings' courts. [26]But what

went ye out for to see? A prophet? Yea, I say
unto you, and much more than a prophet.

**(Luke 7:18-35)**

In this passage we feel the heart beat of John
the Baptist.

The forerunner of the Lord Yeshua, the Messiah,
John the Baptist was a holy man sent from God.
He was sent ahead to declare the arrival of the
Messiah and to point him out to the people and to
the nations. He was the voice to cry in the wilder-
ness, towns and cities, saying,

*"Here He comes!*
*Here He comes!*
*This is the Lamb of God!*
*Who takes away the sins of the world!*
*Happy are those!*
*Who are called to be His friends!*
*Here He comes!*
*Here he comes!*
*The Lamb of God to save your soul!*
*Here He comes!*
*Here he comes!*
*He'll save you and give you rest."*

That was John the Baptist's job description.
So if anyone should know who the Lord Yeshua
was, John the Baptist should. He should be able to
smell him out in a sea of people. He was supposed
to know Him from what he said and from what he

did. One minute, John knew him; the next minute, he was full of doubts. John was full of life, preaching, teaching and baptising and enjoying his banquet of various vegetables, locusts and honey that made some city dwellers want to vomit. But that did not bother him one bit. He was focused, full of the spirit and ready to declare the Master any minute now.

As a Jew born into a Jewish family, John the Baptist must have heard so much of what the enemies of the Jews had done to their people that he began to look and to seek for something else in the Lord Yeshua other than what He came to do. His mindset of what he expected the Lord ought to do started to show.

He sent two of his disciples to go and enquire from the Lord Yeshua, *"Are you the Messiah we are expecting, or shall we start looking for another? Are you the God that our people have put all their trust in all these years to send them a deliverer or shall we start looking elsewhere for our help?"*

The disciples were gentle, obedient souls; otherwise they would have said to him, "Sir, what are we looking for?" I believe that is what God is asking you today: "What are you looking for?"

When you approach God, what are you looking for? What are your expectations? When he acts contrary to your way of thinking, do you get angry, impatient and look elsewhere?

Be patient with God and ask yourself, "What am I looking for?" It is what you're looking for that will determine your attitude and your relationship with God – and as to whether you're going to be patient with God or not.

John was a prophet, someone that God spoke to and someone who interpreted the mind of God. He could go to God in prayer and consultation. However, the circumstances in his life were so severe that he could not believe that God was still the same God. *"Am I seeing right? Am I hearing right? Could it be I was not called by God after all? The way I am looking at things, if I was called by God this would not be happening to me. I know what they are all saying out there. If he was a man of God, this and that should not be happening to him."*

We become judge and jury against ourselves and against God. So you see why John lost his patience and started thinking of looking for another deliverer.

### What was he looking for?

John the Baptist, the fiery preaching prophet, the cousin of the miracle-working, leper-healing, dead-raising Yeshua, had been put into prison and was about to be beheaded.

You're probably still asking, 'What was he looking for?' If you were in his position, what would you be looking for? He was looking for **the Deliverer.** He was looking for a saviour, a conquering Messiah; one who would just say the word and all the enemies of the Jews would fall down and be buried alive!

He was looking for the prison doors to open, his chains to fall off, and his oppressors to be punished. It is natural to expect these, but none of them happened.

"I am His forerunner; I believe in him, I am a believer. I am his kinsman, his own cousin, his flesh and blood. Why am I languishing in jail? Why am I suffering for speaking out against this evil regime? He was supposed to wipe out evil. I am speaking out against evil. He's quite capable of releasing me, but he is letting me rot in here. I am confused – if he can't save me, who then can? Please go and find out. Ask Him. *"Are you the Expected One or shall we start expecting someone else? Have I wasted my time? Have I wasted my life?"*

The Lord then replied John the Baptist with a list of evidence and what should be expected, that is, the real job description of the expected Messiah. He wanted John to compare that list with what he had, and then compare that with what he should already know about the coming Messiah. Then he should make up his own mind.

> [22]Then Jesus answering said unto them, Go your way, and tell John what things ye have seen and heard; how that the blind see, the lame walk, the lepers are cleansed, the deaf hear, the dead are raised, to the poor the gospel is preached. [23]And blessed is he, whosoever shall not be offended in me.

**(Luke 7:22,23)**

"Have a look, cousin John; this is what the Messiah has come to do."

Let us pray:

*Our Father God who made the galaxies*
*And made us humans live and rule like kings*
*Our learning need to get some -ologies*
*Of who you are and how you do your things*

*Certainly all our thoughts are not like yours*
*Nor all our ways the same as all your ways*
*We see the heavens far above the earth*
*Just like your ways are far above our ways*

*We think our thoughts and think we know it all*
*Your thoughts we cannot touch the depths at all.*
*Our Father God, have mercy when we err*
*We mould and try to fix you in our spheres*

*Show mercy Lord; like when we call your name*
*Without the patience to apply your ways*
*Impatient doubts will rise and spread like fame*
*Till lack of faith will bring us down to shame*

*Be Patient with God – What are you looking for?*

Luke 7:23-35

From the last proceedings we saw how human beings can get impatient with God. We want what we want **now**. If possible, we want it yesterday. We also saw that it is not just a weakness of the carnal or insignificant people of this world. Impatience and doubt plagued even the foremost men of God. Even John the Baptist was not left out, though he was the last prophet of the Old Testament; that voice of one crying in the wilderness, telling us about the coming king and the coming new kingdom.

He was the one who ushered in the era of the new dispensation. No wonder the Lord Yeshua said of him in verse 28, *"Among those that are born of women there is not a greater prophet than John the Baptist – but he that is least in the Kingdom of God is greater than he."* John the Baptist was this great and mighty in the Lord, yet he had doubts and he was impatient with God.

Do you see yourself in that picture? The Lord says in verse 23 *"Blessed, happy and highly favoured are those, whosoever they may be, prophets, teachers, pastors, men, women, children – who will not be upset with me."* Those who will not be upset with God for not doing things the way they expect Him to do them or when they expect him to do them. The Lord Yeshua is saying, *"Be patient with God. What more do you want?"* Just say, "May your will be done."

The Lord Yeshua saw that impatience and doubt was rampant in the world. He responded and exclaimed, "What more do you want? What more can I do to prove myself to you? What more can I do for you to put your faith in me?"

Jesus says to you, *"My dearly beloved, what more do you want? What more can I do for you to see my love?"*

Let's take a reading from **Luke 7:29-35**

[29]And when all the people heard Him, even the tax collectors justified God, (agreed and acknowledged that God's way was better) having been baptized with the baptism of John. [30]But the Pharisees and lawyers rejected the will of God for themselves, not having been baptized by him. [31]And the Lord said, "To what then shall I liken the men of this generation, and what are they like? [32]They are like children sitting in the marketplace and calling to one another, saying: 'We played the flute for you, And you did not dance; We mourned to you, And you did not weep.' [33]For John the Baptist came neither eating bread nor drinking wine, and you say, 'He has a demon.' [34]The Son of Man has come eating and drinking, and you say, 'Look, a glutton and a winebibber, a friend of tax collectors and sinners!' [35]But wisdom is justified by all her children."

**(Luke 7:29-35)**

The way it is hard to please the world today is the same way it was hard to please the world when our Lord Yeshua was ministering upon the earth. There were many fault-finders, people who were not interested in the good He did but were more interested in finding fault with everything He did. The Lord was astonished at them; almost screaming out, "What more do you want?"

Verse 29 tells us that it was not everyone that did not believe. Many people believed, including the publicans i.e. tax collectors, whom society had written off and branded as sinners.

Verse 30 says the Pharisees and the lawyers rejected what he was teaching. For the sake of pride, they were willing to lose out on God's plan and purpose for their lives.

The Lord Yeshua rebuked them. He saw them as a fault-finding generation who were very hard to please. The Lord used the imagery of children to explain how difficult it was to please them.

Children are usually honest, simple, uncomplicated and believable, but in the illustration the Lord compares the Pharisees and the lawyers with a hard-to-please set of children whose friends have been trying to get to enjoy the music and merriment of life with them, but they have sniffed at and rejected their overtures.

The illustration was set in the marketplace; meaning that everything was done in the open. There was nothing secret or hidden.

*"What more do you want from me,"* says the Lord. *"I spoke in the open bringing good news of great joy to all mankind, you rejected good news. If I mourn and tell you of the calamities that are going to befall you or Jerusalem; you would not believe me either. What more do you want from me?"*

Verse 33-35

"I tried something different from the prophet, John the Baptist. When he came, he was separate from the whole of society. He ate his own designer brand of food – locusts and wild honey, as God commanded him. His dressing was out of fashion as well. He did not seek fame, fortune or favour but you did not like him. You said he was possessed by a demon.

I have come eating and drinking with everyone, dressing up in what you would call normal, making overtures to everyone (including yourselves) to come and become friends with God and you would have none of it. You rejected John and his baptism and now you are rejecting me, saying that I am a glutton and drinker of wine, a friend of tax collectors and sinners, What more can I do? I cannot describe you any other way than to say that you are an evil and unrepentant generation – very hard to please."

Repent and call on the name of the Lord today and you will be saved. Accept God's plan for your life. Receive his grace and love. Rejoice evermore – only, be patient with God, if you're going to enjoy your life with Him.

In verse 35, the Lord concludes by saying something profound and wonderful to the lawyers and the pharisees.

He said: ***"But wisdom is justified by all her children."***

Here the Lord was using metaphoric language to communicate to the so-called learned people. He personified wisdom and made it a living being, like a child-bearing woman. He taught that every choice we make in life bears its own fruits. Every choice we make has consequences, fruit or children.

The results we get are the children or fruit born out of the choices we make, whether good or bad. These results are what determine whether we made the right decisions or not. Here the Lord was saying to the Pharisees and the Lawyers,

"You think you've made the right decision by rejecting me and my teachings; you think you're wise and have made the wise choice but in the end we'll see if you've been wise by the choice you made. We'll see what fruit or children your choices have borne you, whether you were right or whether I have been right all along. By then it will be too late for you to change your minds."

May it not be too late for you to change your mind today and accept the Lord's teaching and God's plan and purpose for your life, in Yeshua's name. Amen.

# 8

# GOD, THE
# GREATEST SEER

———cvcvcv———

## Luke 7:36-50

In this section, I intend to declare to you the awesomeness of the all-powerful, all-seeing God. I declare to you that our God is the Greatest Seer.

Let's have a look below at the text:

> 36And one of the Pharisees desired him that he would eat with him. And he went into the Pharisee's house, and sat down to meat. 37And, behold, a woman in the city, which was a sinner, when she knew that Jesus sat at meat in the Pharisee's house, brought an alabaster box of ointment, 38And stood at his feet behind him weeping, and began to wash his feet with tears, and did wipe them with the hairs of her head, and kissed his feet, and anointed them with the ointment. 39Now when the Pharisee which had bidden him saw it, he spake within himself, saying, This man, if he

were a prophet, would have known who and what manner of woman this is that toucheth him: for she is a sinner. [40]And Jesus answering said unto him, Simon, I have somewhat to say unto thee. And he saith, Master, say on. [41]There was a certain creditor which had two debtors: the one owed five hundred pence, and the other fifty. [42]And when they had nothing to pay, he frankly forgave them both. Tell me therefore, which of them will love him most? [43]Simon answered and said, I suppose that he, to whom he forgave most. And he said unto him, Thou hast rightly judged. [44]And he turned to the woman, and said unto Simon, Seest thou this woman? I entered into thine house, thou gavest me no water for my feet: but she hath washed my feet with tears, and wiped them with the hairs of her head. [45]Thou gavest me no kiss: but this woman since the time I came in hath not ceased to kiss my feet. [46]My head with oil thou didst not anoint: but this woman hath anointed my feet with ointment. [47]Wherefore I say unto thee, Her sins, which are many, are forgiven; for she loved much: but to whom little is forgiven, the same loveth little. [48]And he said unto her, Thy sins are forgiven. [49]And they that sat at meat with him began to say within themselves, Who is this that forgiveth sins also? [50]And he said to the woman, Thy faith hath saved thee; go in peace.

**(Luke 7:36-50)**

The God we worship is a 'Seer'. He sees things right from the start to the very end. He sees everything from inside out - including the bits we cannot see. He sees a thing from east to west, from north to south and even back to front.

He knew when you were conceived. He knew when you were born and he knows where you are now. That's why He is God. That's why you cannot deceive Him or pull a wool over his eyes. He is God, the Greatest Seer. God saw the world before he created it. We were created in His image and by his grace he appoints some of us his children and his servants, from time to time, to be seers. Those so appointed are able to see things when they are happening or before they happen.

Let's look at some examples before we come back to our text in Luke 7:36-50.

When God sent Moses to Pharaoh, he knew it would be tough. He saw what Pharaoh would do, so he sent Moses with counter awesome power in order to win and be victorious. God sees situations as they are happening and says to you "Fear not, I am still on the throne. I am in control. I am here for you."

He can see "Pharaoh's army" even before you realise that they are pursuing you and provides a way of escape. He fights your battles without you realising it. Put your trust in him, knowing he plans our lives for good. He says in Jeremiah 29:11, *"I know the thoughts that I think towards you, a thought of peace, not of evil, to give you an expected end."*

The Bible also says in Proverbs 3:6-7, *"In all thy ways acknowledge Him and He shall direct thy paths. Be not wise in thy own understanding, fear the Lord, and depart from evil."*

*The Lord our God is the Greatest Seer of all.*
*He sees everything physically*
*He sees everything emotionally*
*He sees everything spiritually*
*He sees far beyond our senses*

Another example is the story of Jonah, the runaway prophet.

He disobeyed God because he knew the people of Nineveh were not just sinners; they were full of iniquity and therefore deserved to pay their due wages, which was death. Perhaps the prophet Jonah prayed some *"dangerous prayers"* where *'die, die'* and *'May they be buried alive'* was attached at the end. I don't know how he concluded it but if it was today it would certainly be concluded with "in Jesus' Name!!!" with a loud shout of "Amen!"

Jonah could not see any good in the people of Nineveh. He could not see why they should live. So, you can imagine the great shock to his system when God said,

*"Go and preach to **that great city,** per adventure they will hear you, repent and I will forgive them."*
*"Who, Who, Sir?*
*You must be kidding me.*
*What did you call them?*
*What did you see in them?*
*You see in them a great city!?*

*That's not what I see.*
*Who's kidding who here?*
*And who's tripping here?"*
And God said,
*"Yeah, yeah, get on with it, Jonah.*
*Do I look like I am kidding?*
*Do I look like I am tripping?*
*I see a fabulous city there.*
*I am the Greatest Seer.*
*My eyes are not like Jonah's*

God's way of seeing is not our way. He sees the good in you even when others cannot see it. He knows what qualities you have and what you are capable of - no matter what others think. Nonetheless, you will be what He has planned for you only if you can stick closer to Him. Then, he will begin to bring them all out of you one by one.

Verse 36
Everyone was joining the bandwagon to say they knew Jesus, that they had met him and had even had dinner with him. People were inviting him left, right and centre, including those who hated him and did not believe in Him - the Scribes, the Pharisees and the Sadducees.

God knows and sees everything. Even before the Pharisees invited Him, He knew their motives. He is our God and he is the Greatest Seer but the Pharisees did not know this.

As you read this book, God is the Greatest Seer who sees everything. He sees you right now and knows whether you are a child of God or not; whether you've been truly born again or you're just playing at being a Christian because you are a member of a certain church organisation. Whatever you have ever considered in your heart, God knows and God sees.

Verses 37-38

In this story we see a woman of the city whom everyone knew to be a sinner. She would not have crossed the threshold to come into the host's house if not for the sake of the Lord Yeshua. The Lord saw exceptional qualities in her which others could not see. She was a sinner, alright. But she was unashamedly repentant. She was a sinner, but she was deeply penitent and contrite in her heart. The Lord Yeshua could see that but the Pharisees had a one-track mind. "She is a sinner who is already condemned to perish."

A street woman's pride is in her makeup and adornment. What did she see in the Lord Yeshua to make her ditch her pride? What did she see in Him to make her weep publicly and ruin her mascara? What on earth could make her ruin her hair and her make-up?

I believe she must have seen in Him the awesomeness of the Greatest Seer of all; One who sees and knows our sins and our shortcomings, but still looks through his eyes of love to forgive us.

*Yeshua, the Greatest Seer, saw her great humility.*
*She kissed his feet with which He walked on dirt.*
*Affirming here that she was low, as low as dust.*
*The dust that man and beast would thread upon each day.*

She was humble, God could see; but people were judgmental. As humans, they could only see with their physical eyes; they could not see what God saw.

Verse 39

The Lord Yeshua did not just go in to eat. He was always looking for an opportunity or an illustration to teach with.

The Pharisee who was his host spoke in the secret place of his heart where no one could see or hear. But God the Greatest Seer saw and responded to his thoughts.

What about you? What about us? Do we sometimes think deep in our hearts, *"It's only me that thinks these thoughts? It's only me that knows. It's only me that hears my thoughts."*

Have you ever found yourself speaking with someone who is physically there with you but is miles away in their thought? You ask them what they're thinking; they reply you with, "nothing." As human as you are, you know for sure that the answer was wrong. They have been thinking a whole lot of things that they are not willing to share with you. Those thoughts may be hidden from you but they're not hidden from the Greatest Seer.

This is therefore teaching us a big lesson as can also be found in one of my songs taken from Philippians 4:8:

*Finally brethren:*
*Whatsoever things are true*
*Whatsoever things are honest*

*Whatsoever things are just*
*Finally brethren:*
*Whatsoever things are pure*
*Whatsoever things are lovely*
*Whatsoever things are of good report*
*If there be any virtue.*
*If there be any praise.*
*Think on these things.*

You might think no one else hears or sees what you are thinking about, but God does.

In this story, the Lord Yeshua's host was thinking: *"If this man was a prophet as he claims to speak the mind of God; if he was really a prophet, he would have seen that prophets are also seers. . ."*

Point of correction: our human prophets are seers only sometimes. They don't see all the time or hear all the time either. They see and hear what God wants them to see and hear, when He wants them to see and when He wants them to hear it. Prophets are only interpreters.

The Lord Yeshua, on the other hand, is more than a prophet. He had seen and knew the deeds of this woman but has chosen to love and forgive her repentant heart. It's easier for God to forgive and forget your sins than for human beings to accept that you have genuinely changed. They could not understand how a harlot could change and become a saint overnight.

*"Look, look, look; she's actually touching him in public. What on earth are they trying to do?"* As his host dwelt on these thoughts, the Lord the Greatest Seer was watching.

Read verses 40-43

At this point, the Lord had to illuminate his thoughts by telling him a story. He told him a parable which was like saying,

*"Figure it out yourself. I am not saying any more about this woman. You figure it out yourself, Simon. She has found something really more precious than all her previous precious things put together. She has found the forgiveness and love of God. And they are:*

*More important to her than her beauty*
*More important to her than her wealth*
*More important to her than her fame*
*More important to her than her pride.*
*She lavished it all on me.*
*Whatever meant so much to her in the past,*
*She lavished it all out on me.*
*What have you lavished on me, Simon?"*

My brother or my sister reading this book, be careful what you think or say because the Seer knows the truth. The Seer also sees all things. You can say you have repented. You can even sing, "I Surrender all." You can also join the throng to the altar but the Seer can see all things. Only He alone can say "Thy sins are forgiven thee" And whosoever the Son sets free then becomes free indeed.

Read verse 50

And he said to the woman, Thy faith hath saved thee; go in peace.

**(Luke 7:50)**

The Bible tells us that out of the abundance of the heart the mouth speaks. You are the thoughts that are in your heart. It is what is in your heart that renews your mind one way or the other.

So, what is in your mind? Do you love the Lord Yeshua such that you are willing to invite Him into your heart to be your Saviour and friend forever? Do you see Him as the Pearl of Greatest Price that makes you willing to throw away all your precious things and see them as dung so that you can have the Lord as the greatest treasure you've ever found? What is on your mind right now? Faith or fear?

I would encourage you to get up and take a step of faith. He will see your heart and grant you His peace and His pardon that surpasses any other thing you've ever known. He will open your heart and your eyes. He will make you a seer too.

# LUKE CHAPTER 8

---

# 9

# THE SOWER WENT OUT TO SOW

—◦∽∾∽◦—

(Luke 8:1-18)

T he above statement sounds so obvious and easy to understand that it can easily be taken for granted. Everyone who hears it will say, "Yes, that is understandable;"

*He was a sower*
*So he went out to sow*
*He was a footballer*
*So he went out to play football*
*He was a fisherman*
*So he went out to fish*
*He was an engineer*
*So he went out to do engineering*
*He was an accountant*
*So he went out to do accounting*
*So, what's the big deal*
*— "a sower went out to sow"?*

When the Lord Yeshua, the Messiah, is the one telling the story, you had better sit up properly to listen and learn!

Verses 1-3

[1]And it came to pass afterward, that he went throughout every city and village, preaching and shewing the glad tidings of the kingdom of God: and the twelve were with him, [2]And certain women, which had been healed of evil spirits and infirmities, Mary called Magdalene, out of whom went seven devils, [3]And Joanna the wife of Chuza Herod's steward, and Susanna, and many others, which ministered unto him of their substance.

The story in Luke 8 verses 1-3 gives us an introductory picture of how the Lord was preaching everywhere in Galilee and afterwards he started going from city to city. There were of course, the synagogues as well as the temple but most of his ministrations were outdoors—in the streets, at the park, on the beach, on the hills and a few times inside the "church." He also went to church regularly on the days of worship. (By 'church' here, I mean the synagogue or the temple).

Whenever He was preaching or teaching, miracles, signs and wonders would follow, to the extent that the news of His teaching would spread in all the lands. People came from far and near to hear him and to see His wonderful deeds.

*He was a big celebrity*
*He had great integrity*
*He did not lack credibility*
*Like today's celebrities.*

Let's look at verse 1,
*He went from place to place*
*Preaching the kingdom of God*
*He went from place to place*
*Establishing the rule of God*
*Like our Lord, it's the kingdom of God*
*Nothing else should matter.*

*Preaching the good news, regarding the love of God.*
*Preaching the good news such as the mercy of God*
*Preaching the good news, like the faithfulness of God.*
*Preaching grace, the unmerited favour of God.*

In verse 3, the Bible tells us who was there at the time.

1. The apostles were there.
2. Mary of Magdala or Mary Magdalene, as we have come to know her, was there.
3. Joanna, the wife of Chuza (Herod's steward) was there, along with Susanna and many more other people.

These people were singled out not only because they've been saved and brought into the kingdom, but because they have now become true followers, following him night and day. They were showing their gratitude to God by contributing their means to the spreading of the Gospel.

*They were no longer mere Christians;*
*They had become disciples.*
*They were no longer bench-warmers in church;*
*They had become disciples.*
*They may not be the twelve,*
*But they were true disciples.*
*They had evolved and are involved*
*Gone from what the Lord would do for them*
*To "what shall we do for our Lord?"*

The Bible tells us in verse 3 that there were many of them "who were contributing to the support of the work, out of their private means. With this support, the Lord and his disciples were able to go to more and more cities to preach the government and kingdom of God.

Dearly beloved, I don't know who you are. Whether you are rich or poor, young or old, male or female, black, white or any other colour, God needs your wholehearted support for the expansion of His rule on earth. He can do it without you but He wants you to be part of His divine mission.

Just as in the days of our Lord Yeshua when He was physically here on earth, even more so it is today. Expansion of course, will attract a great mixed multitude.

Let's have a look at verses 4-9.

[4]And when much people were gathered together, and were come to him out of every city, he spake by a parable: [5]A sower went out to sow his seed: and as he sowed, some fell by the way side; and it was trodden down, and the fowls of the air devoured it. [6]And some fell upon a rock; and as soon as it was sprung up, it withered away, because it lacked moisture. [7]And some fell among thorns; and the thorns sprang up with it, and choked it. [8]And other fell on good ground, and sprang up, and bare fruit an hundredfold. And when he had said these things, he cried, He that hath ears to hear, let him hear. [9]And his disciples asked him, saying, What might this parable be?

All kinds of people were touched. Some became supporters, workers and helpers. Some became apostles while others became disciples. There was also the 'great multitude'. Each person there came for their own specific reasons.

Look at verses 4-9 again. The Lord Yeshua is saying to us as He told them at the time,

*"It's not enough to follow me about the way you follow celebrities dishing out entertainment. I am here to bring you the good news and to establish the rule of God.*

*Hello! Is anyone in there? (Knocking on their skulls).*

*Are the words I am speaking making sense to anyone? Is it going in or am I speaking to myself?"*

*Sometimes you labour, preach and teach*
*Travailing with a push.*
*You've done your bit, "It is as clear as day."*
*You come to find, it's not the case*
*Some have not understood.*

Even the disciples did not understand Him. The Lord made them understand that it was a privilege for them to hear what they were hearing and see what they were seeing.

The Lord Yeshua wants you to understand today that what you're hearing or seeing, either from this book or from other Christian books, but most especially from the Bible, is privileged information made available to the children of God. It is a privilege that you have ears to hear Him and a heart to understand.

The Bible tells us in verse 8 that as He narrated those parables to the multitude or to His disciples, He would cry or call out, "He who has ears to hear these things, let him hear." The shout out from the Lord has been echoing through the ages and has reached you and I today.

The Lord was observing the different kinds of people coming and going. He could see people as He was sowing spiritual seed and establishing the kingdom of God. He saw that there were people:

· who were taking the whole thing lightly, like a picnic or entertainment.
· who were hard at heart and even despised the Word. They were careless with their lives or couldn't care less.

- that were emotional hearers, emotional at the point of hearing but unstable in their hearts.
- that had preoccupied minds, choked by the cares of this world.

Now, this categorisation referred to people in Bible times. However, as far as you are concerned, where do you fit? Where has the seed of the Word of God fallen in your heart?

*The Sower went out to sow*
*Some fell by the road side*
*Some fell on a rocky soil*
*Others fell among the thorns*
*And others fell on the good soil*

He is still sowing His seed. When it falls, where will it fall for you? On the wayside, trampled upon, disrespected and abused? Or is it on a hard, rocky heart, not nourished by faith, hope and charity? Is it on a busy-body, do-gooder, friends'-pleaser heart that has no time for the seed, the word of God to germinate and flourish? Which one will it be? Or will you today purposely fertilise your heart as the good soil, where the word of God can germinate, grow and bear fruit? Let's read verses 11-15 as the Lord explains the parable.

[11]Now the parable is this: The seed is the word of God.

[12]Those by the way side are they that hear; then cometh the devil, and taketh away the word out of their hearts, lest they should believe and be saved. [13]They on the rock are they, which, when they hear, receive the word with joy; and these have no root, which for a while believe, and in time of temptation fall away.

[14]And that which fell among thorns are they, which, when they have heard, go forth, and are choked with cares and riches and pleasures of this life, and bring no fruit to perfection. [15]But that on the good ground are they, which in an honest and good heart, having heard the word, keep it, and bring forth fruit with patience.

**(Luke 8:11-15)**

In verse 9 we realise that even the disciples did not understand the parables. He was trying to make them understand that the word of God is not just ordinary words. It is deep, it is spirit and it gives life. However, to **anyone** who has an open heart to hear and receive it, it is a privilege.

In verses 11-15 above, he explains the parable. There were many that came to hear him. If you were there, which kind of person would you have been? Which kind of soil (heart) would you be? I pray today that you chose to make your heart the good soil to receive the word in Yeshua's name. Amen.

Verses 16-18

<sup>16</sup>No man, when he hath lighted a candle, covereth it with a vessel, or putteth it under a bed; but setteth it on a candlestick, that they which enter in may see the light. <sup>17</sup>For nothing is secret, that shall not be made manifest; neither any thing hid, that shall not be known and come abroad. <sup>18</sup>Take heed therefore how ye hear: for whosoever hath, to him shall be given; and whosoever hath not, from him shall be taken even that which he seemeth to have.

**(Luke 8:16-18)**

If you have seen the light, you cannot be in darkness.

If you have been lit up, you cannot be hidden. People will see it in you and they will gravitate to your light. The question is:

*Are you a Christian?*
*Have you seen the light?*
*Are you lit up by the Word?*
*Are people able to see it?*

If you've caught it, go spread it. It is the good news of great joy to all mankind and it cannot be hidden. One thing is for sure: Christianity is no secret society.

Verse 18 says it's all about how you listen. How do you listen and for what motive? When you hear the Word of God, how do you hear it? What do you make of it? How passionately and how purposefully do you hear it?

Verse eighteen says:

*The more you seek it*
*The more you find it*
*The more you get it*
*The more it will shine out of you*
*The more you receive the Word*
*The more you'll be blessed*
*With the power that is in the Word.*
*Take heed therefore how you hear it today*
*For the Sower has gone out to sow.*

Here is my prayer for you:

*And may the seed fall on good soil in your heart today*
*The kingdom of God being established in your heart today*
*May His loving, merciful face shine upon you today*
*May He give you peace as you open your heart today*
*In the Lord Yeshua's name. Amen.*

## 10

# WHO IS THIS MAN, YESHUA?

———◦◦◦———

(Luke 8:20-40)

Sometimes, when you hear people talking about the Lord Yeshua, you would think they just had tea with him this morning; or they were playing golf with him just yesterday evening; or that they know him far better than anybody else and that they could write a far better Da-Vinci-code about him. Unfortunately, in the end, it all becomes vanity upon vanity and vexation of spirit, especially where it was all done in the flesh. That's why, at this juncture, I would like us to examine the topic, **'Who is this man, Yeshua?'**

He is your pal and you might eat with him all the time, but he does things that fascinates me and makes him an enigma; hard to fully understand.

Or, perhaps you've never really known him. This study will really make you think and say "Wow, you are the Lord Yeshua and my God!"

Our text is Luke 8:20-40.

[20]And it was told Him by some, who said, "Your mother and Your brothers are standing outside, desiring to see You." [21]But He answered and said to them, "My mother and My brothers are these who hear the word of God and do it." [22]Now it happened, on a certain day, that He got into a boat with His disciples. And He said to them, "Let us cross over to the other side of the lake." And they launched out. [23]But as they sailed He fell asleep. And a windstorm came down on the lake, and they were filling with water, and were in jeopardy. [24]And they came to Him and awoke Him, saying, "Master, Master, we are perishing!" Then He arose and rebuked the wind and the raging of the water. And they ceased, and there was a calm. [25]But He said to them, "Where is your faith?" And they were afraid, and marveled, saying to one another, "Who can this be? For He commands even the winds and water, and they obey Him!" [26]Then they sailed to the country of the Gadarenes, which is opposite Galilee. [27]And when He stepped out on the land, there met Him a certain man from the city who had demons for a long time. And he wore no clothes, nor did he live in a house but in the tombs. [28]When he saw Jesus, he cried out, fell down before Him, and with a loud voice said, "What have I to do with You, Jesus, Son of the Most High God? I beg You, do not torment me!" [29]For He had commanded the unclean spirit to come out of the man. For it

had often seized him, and he was kept under guard, bound with chains and shackles; and he broke the bonds and was driven by the demon into the wilderness. [30]Jesus asked him, saying, "What is your name?" And he said, "Legion," because many demons had entered him. [31]And they begged Him that He would not command them to go out into the abyss. [32]Now a herd of many swine was feeding there on the mountain. So they begged Him that He would permit them to enter them. And He permitted them. [33]Then the demons went out of the man and entered the swine, and the herd ran violently down the steep place into the lake and drowned. [34]When those who fed them saw what had happened, they fled and told it in the city and in the country. [35]Then they went out to see what had happened, and came to Jesus, and found the man from whom the demons had departed, sitting at the feet of Jesus, clothed and in his right mind. And they were afraid. [36]They also who had seen it told them by what means he who had been demon-possessed was healed. [37]Then the whole multitude of the surrounding region of the Gadarenes asked Him to depart from them, for they were seized with great fear. And He got into the boat and returned. [38]Now the man from whom the demons had departed begged Him that he might be with Him. But Jesus sent him away, saying, [39]"Return to your own house, and tell what great things God has done for you." And he went his way and proclaimed throughout the whole city what great things Jesus had done for him. [40]So it was, when Jesus returned, that the multitude welcomed Him, for they were all waiting for Him.

**(Luke 8:20-40)**

After reading verses 20-21, what would you say? Was the Lord Yeshua a disrespectful person who hated his mother and despised his brothers and sisters? On the contrary, he was a lover of people, including Mary, his mother and his brothers and sisters. But the way he responded here, you would think that he did not respect them.

We can see that the Lord Yeshua anticipated what would happen after he had gone. He knew that people could set up companies of 'Been-With-And-Known-Yeshua Enterprises Ltd.' These would be businesses that distract people from the real thing, bringing them fame and fortune in the name of the Lord, but not really knowing the Lord. So what would you say for yourself today?

One of our church elders, Laurence Alozie, wrote a song many years ago. The chorus started with a question and answer:

*Do you know the Lord ?*
*Oh yes I know the Lord*
*He's the living God*
*Whose name is Jehovah.*

The Lord knew that if he did not stop it there and then, the time would come (and we are in that time right now) when people would worship the brothers and sisters of the Lord more than the Lord himself. People will elevate honour and venerate everything else to do with the Lord Yeshua, rather than the Lord himself. He knew that would happen and isn't it happening in our world today? Mary, the mother of the Lord Yeshua is given the greatest honour in some quarters - more than the Lord Yeshua is given. Some feasts relating to Yeshua, such as Christmas and Easter, are now more important than Yeshua himself.

So he took time on that day to correct that mistake. "My mother and my brothers are those who hear the word of God and do it."

1. God is no respecter of persons.
2. The word of God is far more important than mother, father, brother or sister.
3. Your relationship with God must be a personal thing. You cannot stand aloof on the outside and expect God to come and meet you because of your privileged position. God is no respecter of persons.

My brother or my sister, you need God. Without him, you can do absolutely nothing. You need to get close to him, hear his word and purpose in your heart that you will do it. Then, you will be his special friend.

So, who's this man, Yeshua?

Let us go over to the other side of the lake and have a look at the rest of the story from verse 22.

The word of God says that a great wind descended upon them and they were in danger. They came to him and woke him up saying, "Master, Master, we're perishing." The question is, when you are facing hardship and difficulties, who are you going to call? Will you call on the Lord, the Master of the wind or would you call on ghostbusters? May the Lord rebuke your gale force wind, in Yeshua's name. Amen. May he rebuke your difficulties, your trials and temptations in Yeshua's name. Amen.

Verse 24
He arose, rebuked the wind and the waves and everything became calm. He turned to his disciples and asked them, "Where is your faith?" They were even more afraid and wondered, "Who is this man, that even the wind and the waves, obey him?" They were with him morning, noon and night. They probably played games with him, went fishing with him, shared packed lunches with him and even played in the park with him.

He was friendly, yet not too familiar. He was down to earth, yet not too earthy. He was kind and respectful but he did not fail to tell people the truth, irrespective of who they were. That's who the Lord Yeshua is.

He says today, "You need the word of God. You must know that faith comes by hearing and hearing by the word of God. Without faith, it's impossible to please God." In the passage above, He says to you and I today, as He said to His disciples over two thousand years ago, "Where is your faith?"

So Who's This Man, Yeshua?

Sometimes in the Bible, we hear verses that fascinate us, but we never actually see typical examples of it. Jesus said in John 10:10, "The devil has come for to kill, to steal and to destroy; but I have come to give life, and to give it more abundantly?"

In this passage, verse 24 is a typical example and a fulfilment of that passage.

So, who is this man, Yeshua? Well, He's the one who "*...commands even the winds and water, and they obey Him!*"

In verses 27-38, we read the pathetic story of the man possessed by the devil for many years.

· The devil with his demons had devastated and destroyed him.
· The devil had mocked him. The devil had entombed him.
· He was no longer living with the living. But made his bed with the dead at the grave yard.
· The rest of the world thought he was finished and he believed it too.
· He would have been killed and destroyed completely if he had not met the Lord Yeshua. Because he thought he was finished, it would have been so easy for the devil to finish him off if he had not met the Lord.

A well-known motivational speaker, Charles Emeka, in his book ***Against All Odds***, wrote, "*The issues and battles of life are won and lost in the mind.*

*In all you do, be the best and never forget that you were born to win."* Interesting, isn't it?

In the story of the man who was possessed by the devil and his demons, you could see that the devil had done a thorough job on him. He stole the man's dignity and destroyed his life in order to kill him completely. He would have succeeded if the Lord had not stepped in.

So, who is this man Yeshua?

1. that the demons tremble at the sight of him or at the sound of His voice?
2. that the devil knows, that the demons know, that he has power to destroy them?
3. who has the power to untie and set free people who have been in bondage and chains of the devil?
4. that even the demons have to ask him permission before they could take up a new accommodation?

The point of the lesson in this section is really a question I would like to ask you. The question is, knowing the awesomeness and the power of our Lord Yeshua, knowing who He is and what He's capable of doing, who would you rather be with? The Lord Yeshua who is the Messiah, the Redeemer, the Saviour and the Good Shepherd or Satan the destroyer?

[38]Now the man from whom the demons had departed begged Him that he might be

with Him. But Jesus sent him away, saying, [39]"Return to your own house, and tell what great things God has done for you." And he went his way and proclaimed throughout the whole city what great things Jesus had done for him. [40]So it was, when Jesus returned, that the multitude welcomed Him, for they were all waiting for Him.

**(Luke 8:38-40)**

Demons could not stand him because they are evil; but He is your friend, one who plans to give you an expected end, a future with hope and abundant life.

The demons, as you can see, can assume many forms. They may not come out so ugly with two horns. They may be in the form of a sheep, a goat or any animal. They may also come in the form of the most gorgeous celebrity ever, or an ordinary man in the street and be used by the devil. One thing we must learn is that God has not taken away the devil's capacity to assume any form he chooses.

However, if we seek the Lord and his word to obey it, we have nothing to worry about, no matter what form or disguise the enemy comes in. Just as the pigs were all drowned in the river, the demons and the troubles that trouble you would be drowned by the Lord today, in Yeshua's Name.

Are you getting a glimpse of who Yeshua is? The Bible says that He went about doing good. He came to his own, but his own did not receive him. However, as many as received him, to them gave He power to become children of God. Lots of people from that city came to see him. Did they all receive him? No. Rather, they asked him to depart, preferring great prosperity with their herds to good life and salvation with the Saviour.

Now that you've known who he is and what he is capable of doing, I hope you will make Him your friend today. I hope you will ask him to stay and help you to live your Christian life with great anticipation of a far better life with Him in heaven.

*11*

# LORD, WE ARE MISSING YOU

———❧———

(Luke 8:40–56)

I t is a fact that people do not value what they have when they have them. But when those things are absent (even for a very brief period), they get desperate, as if they would die without them.

This is so true of human relationships when friends and family members so often take each other for granted. It is also true regarding our relationship with God. If we see Him around us all the time, we would quickly start to take Him for granted - which is a very dangerous thing to do.

For a mature believer, the absence of God's presence in his or her life (even for the shortest period of time) is like living in a desert with no oasis or sign of water. The result of this will be death.

In the passage we are about to study, we will see all kinds of people who were waiting for the Lord Yeshua to return. They rushed to welcome Him back, almost exclaiming with excitement, "Lord, We Have

Missed You!" Yet He had been away from them only for a short period of time.

*Let us read it.*

[40]So it was, when Jesus returned, that the multitude welcomed Him, for they were all waiting for Him.[41]And behold, there came a man named Jairus, and he was a ruler of the synagogue. And he fell down at Jesus' feet and begged Him to come to his house, [42]for he had an only daughter about twelve years of age, and she was dying. But as He went, the multitudes thronged Him. [43]Now a woman, having a flow of blood for twelve years, who had spent all her livelihood on physicians and could not be healed by any, [44]came from behind and touched the border of His garment. And immediately her flow of blood stopped. [45]And Jesus said, "Who touched Me?" When all denied it, Peter and those with him said, "Master, the multitudes throng and press You, and You say, 'Who touched Me?'" [46]But Jesus said, "Somebody touched Me, for I perceived power going out from Me." [47]Now when the woman saw that she was not hidden, she came trembling; and falling down before Him, she declared to Him in the presence of all the people the reason she had touched Him and how she was healed immediately. [48]And He said to her, "Daughter, be of good cheer; your faith

has made you well. Go in peace." ⁴⁹While He was still speaking, someone came from the ruler of the synagogue's house, saying to him, "Your daughter is dead. Do not trouble the Teacher." ⁵⁰But when Jesus heard it, He answered him, saying, "Do not be afraid; only believe, and she will be made well." ⁵¹When He came into the house, He permitted no one to go in except Peter, James, and John, and the father and mother of the girl. ⁵²Now all wept and mourned for her; but He said, "Do not weep; she is not dead, but sleeping." ⁵³And they ridiculed Him, knowing that she was dead.

⁵⁴But He put them all outside, took her by the hand and called, saying, "Little girl, arise." ⁵⁵Then her spirit returned, and she arose immediately. And He commanded that she be given something to eat. ⁵⁶And her parents were astonished, but He charged them to tell no one what had happened.

**(Luke 8:40-56)**

The evening before, the Lord decided to cross to the other side of the river where the Gerasenes lived (Luke 8:26). He went there to do what he usually did – teaching, healing, casting out demons and setting people free. He had done these things in Galilee, Capernaum, and Jerusalem and then decided to go over to Gerasene to do the same thing for the people of that country.

Before that evening, people were getting used to Him and familiarity was beginning to breed contempt. They were starting to take him for granted. Some were coming not to listen but only as spectators. They wanted to see what signs and wonders He would perform. If none was forth-coming, they would prompt Him and taunt Him by saying "Show us a sign." He would refuse, of course, because He was not a show-man or one of their clowns who would do one for them at the drop of a hat. So, he left them briefly to go to another country, as the Bible says.

There, He preached to the Gerasenes and delivered people who had been in bondage for many years. One of such was a man in such a pathetic condition that he had to make his home with the dead at the cemetery – thus accepting his fate as a 'living dead'. It is almost like saying, "I am dead anyway, I might as well get nearer and get a space for my burial." The Lord went over there specifically to release him and set him free.

The man was possessed with demons and those demons recognised the Lord. They were afraid of Him and were not sure what He would do to them, so they requested to be allowed to go into the swine that were nearby. Unclean demons went into unclean animals.

Notice that the unclean spirits were asking permission of the Lord before they did anything. The Lord permitted them. The result was chaotic and catastrophic. The swine did not know what hit them. In a panic, they all rushed into the sea and drowned.

The owners were not happy. They did not want the Lord Yeshua around any longer. They saw Him as bad news for their business. They did not know him very well. If they had, they would have made friends with Him and He would have made them abundantly rich. He would have blessed them with more sheep and cattle on every hill than they would have been able to handle. But they kicked Him out.

While the Lord was being kicked out from the country of the Gerasenes, there was a multitude in Galilee who were starved of his presence and were desperate to have him back. These were those who had heard of and known about him and his works and could not wait to have him back again in their lives.

Verse 40 tells us that when he returned, the multitude welcomed Him because they had been waiting for Him. Among the multitude were people who genuinely needed the Lord. There were people with various needs - spiritual as well as physical - who had desperately missed him, like missing water in a hot desert land. You could almost hear their sigh of relief, as if to say, 'Lord, we have missed you.'

Isn't it wonderful to know that while some people are rejecting him today, there are still many others who are desperate for Him? They long for his touch and his presence in their lives. Are you one of them?

From verses **40–45** we notice that a synagogue official needed Him, a sick young girl needed Him, a grown up woman also needed Him; not counting the rest of the multitude who had gathered either to hear Him or just to watch Him do miracles.

My prayer for you is that even if the rest of the world rejects the Lord, you will not be among them and you will not kick him out of your life. Always have that hunger for him in your heart that cries out, "LORD I AM MISSING YOU!"

Back in verse **41** we notice that the synagogue official was not ashamed of the Lord, neither was he afraid of being kicked out of the synagogue for talking to this person whom the Pharisee, the Scribes and the Saducees did not approve of. They saw the Lord as an imposter, an upstart and a blasphemer but the synagogue official saw him as a redeemer, a deliverer and a saviour.

Here we see that the official had needs and he would not leave or stop troubling the Lord until he had got help for his need, irrespective of who was watching. He did not walk away from his help. I pray that you will not walk away from your help. The Lord Yeshua is ready to listen and to help you with your needs today.

In verse **42**, the 12-year old girl who was at the point of death, desperately needed Him. Though the asking was done by her father, if the Lord was not present to be asked, she would have died. She did not die because the Lord Yeshua had already declared that He was the Way, the Truth and the Life. He restores life when it seems as if there's no hope for life. That's His Job. That's his claim. And nowhere else explains this claim to us than this particular story, as well as in the raising of Lazarus from the dead.

I don't know what your situation is or where you are in terms of your relationship with God. Are you almost finished, dead, down and out? Well, the Lord can bring you back to life. It is one of His promises to you.

As you read verse 42 again, I want you to meditate on the fact that besides the synagogue official and his near-death daughter, there was also the multitude. I want to remind you that though the multitude was there, not everyone that was there was able to touch the Lord or were able to be touched by Him. He was available to those who genuinely and desperately were missing Him in their lives.

In verses 43–46 we read the story of a woman with the issue of blood; a woman whose menstrual period had flowed and poured out every day for over 12 years. She was suffering from a dreadful disease: a blood haemorrhage that no one was able to cure. She had been everywhere and seen every doctor imaginable, trying to get help. No one was able to give her life back to her, except the Life-giver Himself. Only the Lord can cure the incurable. Man can cure but only God can heal completely.

This woman with the issue of blood realised this and she purposed in her heart that she was going to brave it through the crowd to touch the Lord Yeshua's garment. The same story is found in Mark chapter 5.

One of the intriguing things in that story was the question the Lord asked: "Who touched me?" Of course, he knew who touched him but he asked because he wants us to testify with our own mouths of the goodness of God in our lives. Imagine what would have happened if he did not ask. Imagine what would have happened if the woman did not own up and testify of what the Lord had done for her.

Don't forget that this woman had been going to the doctors for 12 years to seek a solution to her problem - without any success. Who would have taken the credit for her healing, if she did not own up and testify? Probably the doctors. There would have been lots of arguments as to who actually healed her: the trained doctors or the so-called Rabbi; the medication or the 'miracle healer' who had not even seen or touched the woman but claimed to have healed her.

Remember the argument that ensued after the healing of the man that was born blind? They accused him of lying that he had been born blind in the first place. They even told him, "Give credit to God. We know that this man is a sinner. Come on, tell us the truth. How did you get your sight back, if you say that you were really born blind?"

We learn from these stories that it is good to testify of the goodness of God with our own mouths, from our own hearts, without force or coercion from anyone.

When we testify in public and out of our own volition, it has much power and authority to convince many that God is still at work doing lots of miraculous signs and wonders.

Again, it is good to show our thanks and gratitude to God when he touches us or when we touch him. My encouragement to you is to also own up and confess to the goodness of God in touching your life.

Remember that when you touch God, you will also be touched by him; and when that happens, you'll never be the same again and even your mouth will not be able to keep it quiet.

*Do not be ashamed of Him*
*Do not be afraid of Him*
*By keeping silent you would be stealing from Him.*
*You'll be covering His glory and perhaps*
*Giving that glory to someone else or something*
*else.*

The disciples said to the Lord, "It is impossible to know who touched you; there are thousands of people in this multitude pressing to get near you".

His response was that though there was a great multitude of people pressing on Him, not all of them have really touched him. There were those who had genuinely come to Him. They had touched him and he had touched them by what he said and what he did. Others were merely what I would call 'follow-follow'. They follow the crowd. Wherever there's a big crowd, there you will find them. They may not have heard a word of what was said. They might not even have seen what was done. They just drift along with the crowd, never really committed to what was going on.

The Lord Yeshua says this about people like that: 'They may be in the crowd but they have not even heard a word I said, let alone touch me; but someone has.'

In this story we learn to testify and show gratitude. The question is, why should we show our thanks and gratitude to God for what He has done for us?

The answer is:

1. It makes him happy to know that we are realising and seeing his hand in everything and that nothing is impossible with Him.
2. It makes him happy to do more for us, seeing we are appreciative of his past deeds.
3. It shows that we understand that he is the one who did it.
4. That he is alive as the living God and able to keep his promises.
5. That he hears our prayers and cares for us, even at difficult times when it seems as if he has not answered.
6. It shows that we know that he is the only one who fully understands us spirit, soul and body because he created us.
7. By testifying and giving thanks, we declare that he is good and his mercies endure forever.
8. By testifying and giving thanks, we proclaim that his steadfast love never ceases, that they are new every morning and great is His faithfulness.
9. Most importantly, that we do not attribute His power and glory to another person or thing.

In verses 47-48 we see that there is peace to be had when we 'own up'. That includes regularly confessing our sins and short-comings to the Lord.

The Bible says in 1 John 1:9-10, "If we confess our sins, He is faithful and just to forgive us our sins and to cleanse us from all unrighteousness..." The woman in this story owned up and confessed that she was the one that touched the Lord. She was not ashamed of the Lord, neither was she ashamed of her own physical or spiritual state.

Immediately after her confession, the Lord Yeshua released her and blessed her. He said to her "Daughter, go in peace, your faith has made you well" (Verse 48).

Owning up does not always have to be in negative situations. Besides, what we would see as negative is not negative with God.

The woman was scared. She thought she had done a terrible thing by touching a Rabbi in her "unclean state." She was right. It would have been a terrible thing to do, (in those days) to deliberately go and touch a Rabbi, a priest or any of the religious leaders in her unclean state.

Thank God, the Lord Yeshua is our Great physician and the Great Healer. Sickness has no chance of hanging around while He is around. One of the claims of the Lord Yeshua about himself which He made while He was on the earth was that He was the Resurrection and the Life. This teaches that in our lives, if we need to awake or arise from whatever situation we find ourselves in, we only need to call him.

Since the world began, no one else has ever made such a claim to be "the Resurrection, the Way, the Truth and the Life." We see an example of this by how He gave the woman with the blood disease her life back, thereby resurrecting her and reinstating her back into her community.

Verses 49-50

Here also we see another fulfilment of His claim to be the giver of life. You remember earlier in verse 41 when Jairus needed help from the Lord. His daughter was very sick and "near unto death". Now, here he is told that the girl has actually died. While the Lord was busy dealing with other people's issues, the girl died. Messengers came running up to her father, saying, "Don't bother yourself and don't bother the rabbi any further. Your daughter is dead."

The messengers were natural people and spoke naturally. We cannot blame them for their language or how they delivered the message. After all, they had never seen a situation before where someone who was dead was brought back to life. They probably thought, "If he would help the girl, it would have been while she was alive. Now she is dead, there is not much anyone can do for her.'

Read what the Lord said to the father in verse 50: "Do not be afraid; only believe, and she shall be made well". And that is exactly what happened, as we read further.

Verses 51-56 tells of how the Lord went to Jairus' house and met the people wailing and mourning. Doom and gloom had descended on the family. As far as they were concerned, she was dead and there was nothing more to it. As far as they were concerned, this is not a case of merely changing water into wine or feeding the 5000 with a loaf of bread and a few fish. This was death, and no one could help them.

They were not waiting with anticipation and saying, "Lord, we are missing you. You are what is missing in our lives." No. They had lost all hope.

The Lord Yeshua proved them wrong. The Lord is the resurrection and life. In verse 51, he asked everyone else to get out of the room, except for Peter, James, John and the girl's parents. These were the people who knew him well and the parents who were desperate to have their daughter brought back to life. The rest, as they say, is history.

The best thing to do is for you to read verses 52-56 again, how the Lord went in, called the girl up from her 'sleep' and brought her back to life.

Jairus was probably among the people waiting for the Lord as he returned from the country of the Gerasenes. He was among those who heaved a sigh of relief, saying: "Lord, we are missing you."

Isaiah 40:31 says,

"They that wait upon the Lord shall renew their strength. They shall mount up with wings like eagles. They will run (or they will wait) and not be weary (tired or grow impatient). They will walk (with the Lord) and not faint (or give up).

We all need the Lord everyday of our lives. We cannot afford *not* to have Him in our lives. Even when for a moment it seems as if he has abandoned us or gone away from us, we must keep on seeking and waiting upon him. When he reappears, we shall say, "Lord, we are missing you."

# LUKE CHAPTER 9

---

## 12

# THE ABUNDANT KINGDOM

———⁓⁓⁓———

The Lord Yeshua came to remind us of who we are. Through His life and ministry, he showed us what it meant to be a child of God's Kingdom. This refers to The Abundant Kingdom of God where there is no lack; the Kingdom where you can have whatever you need; where all you need to do is ask.

If what you require is not available in the first place, it will be made for you. God is the Creator and in His Kingdom, every citizen has the capacity, capability, potential and propensity to create by faith, even what does not exist.

Let us take a look at some Scriptures concerning The Abundant Kingdom.

> [1] Then He called His twelve disciples together and gave them power and authority over all demons, and to cure diseases. [2] He sent them to preach the kingdom of God and to heal the sick. [3] And He said to them, "Take nothing

for the journey, neither staffs nor bag nor bread nor money; and do not have two tunics apiece. ⁴"Whatever house you enter, stay there, and from there depart. ⁵And whoever will not receive you, when you go out of that city, shake off the very dust from your feet as a testimony against them." ⁶So they departed and went through the towns, preaching the gospel and healing everywhere.

⁷Now Herod the tetrarch heard of all that was done by Him; and he was perplexed, because it was said by some that John had risen from the dead, 8 and by some that Elijah had appeared, and by others that one of the old prophets had risen again. ⁹Herod said, "John I have beheaded, but who is this of whom I hear such things?" So he sought to see Him.

¹⁰And the apostles, when they had returned, told Him all that they had done. Then He took them and went aside privately into a deserted place belonging to the city called Bethsaida. ¹¹But when the multitudes knew it, they followed Him; and He received them and spoke to them about the kingdom of God, and healed those who had need of healing. ¹²When the day began to wear away, the twelve came and said to Him, "Send the multitude away, that they may go into the surrounding towns and country, and lodge and get provisions; for we are in a deserted

place here." [13]But He said to them, "You give them something to eat." And they said, "We have no more than five loaves and two fish, unless we go and buy food for all these people." [14]For there were about five thousand men. Then He said to His disciples, "Make them sit down in groups of fifty."

[15]And they did so, and made them all sit down. [16]Then He took the five loaves and the two fish, and looking up to heaven, He blessed and broke them, and gave them to the disciples to set before the multitude. [17]So they all ate and were filled, and twelve baskets of the leftover fragments were taken up by them.

[18]And it happened, as He was alone praying, that His disciples joined Him, and He asked them, saying, "Who do the crowds say that I am?" [19]So they answered and said, "John the Baptist, but some say Elijah; and others say that one of the old prophets has risen again." [20]He said to them, "But who do you say that I am?" Peter answered and said, "The Christ of God."

[21]And He strictly warned and commanded them to tell this to no one, [22]saying, "The Son of Man must suffer many things, and be rejected by the elders and chief priests and scribes, and be killed, and be raised the third day."

**(Luke 9:1-22)**

The Abundant Kingdom has power and authority to trouble all your troubles (spiritual or physical). In verses 1-2, we see that man is physical as well as spiritual. Our problems are also either physical or spiritual.

*Preach the kingdom of God*
*Preach the authority of God*
*Preach the rule of God*
*Then the Healing of God*
*Will come from the throne of God.*

Healing (both physical and spiritual) will take place. So go preach and heal, says the Lord."

Verse 3 reveals the scope of abundance in The Abundant Kingdom.

*Don't worry about food*
*Don't worry about money*
*Don't worry about clothing*
*Expect a miracle in your journey.*
*God will provide for the work.*
*Put your trust in him*
*Have faith in him*
*If you want to please him*
*As the angels please him*
*Put your trust in him.*

Verses 4-5 says,

Do not discriminate. Do not show favouritism for the rich over the poor. Some will receive you, some will not. Everything will not be a bed of roses. Don't go looking for the house of the rich when you arrive in a city to preach. If the first house you enter is a poor man's house, stay there; eat and drink whatever is set before you, giving thanks to your host and to God. Do not move and change accommodation to the rich man's house, where you think you may be looked after more sumptuously.

Imagine how you would feel if the great Evangelist Greyhound came to your house for a week-long evangelistic outreach. You were the first person who accommodated him when he had nowhere to lay his head. You have no car and you are not what they would call "rich".

The first two days into the week, you have enjoyed walking with him to and from the venue of the meeting. You and your family have looked after the man of God the best way you could. Before the start of the meeting on the third day, you see a beautiful car pull up in front of your house with a man and a woman in the front seats tooting their car horn. Your guest now tells you that Mr. and Mrs. Affluence have come to pick him up for lunch.

If he then turns around as he enters the car, puts his luggage on the back seat of the car and tells you he might be staying with Mr. and Mrs. Affluence for the rest of his stay, how would you feel? Hurt and betrayed, of course! Moreover, Mr. and Mrs. Affluence are already well to do, why would they deny you of the privilege of looking after the man of God? That is why the Lord warned His disciples not to do it, as it would be blatant discrimination and favouritism.

Wherever you first find hospitality, stay there; unless of course, it is the wish of your hosts that you find a more comfortable place.

Verse 6

Again, preaching, teaching and healing do not depend on any human being. It depends on God, the owner of the Abundant Kingdom. (Read verses 7-9).

The Abundant Kingdom brings fear to unbelievers, even the most powerful people. Because the world is untrustworthy, they find it hard to trust anyone else. They are scared of the doctrine of resurrection. Could the dead come back to life? Could the people they had once hurt come back to haunt or hurt them?

Unbelievers believe that "seeing is believing." The Abundant Kingdom is a kingdom of faith, miracles, signs and wonders. Therefore the Abundant Kingdom goes against their grain, against the tide of their river of thought.

Many came to the Lord Yeshua just because they wanted to see Him. Even Herod had been wanting to see Him.

Verses 10-12

The Twelve were observant and compassionate. They noticed that the people were tired and hungry. The solution they had was for the Lord to send them away so they could look after themselves. They knew the Lord Yeshua could do miracles, but they did not imagine he could do one of this magnitude - cater for five thousand people. In their head, they knew that their Master could do whatever he chose to do, but it never occurred to them that "whatever" he chose to do could include multiplying food to feed a multitude of people. They did not know that He was teaching them about the Abundant Kingdom.

They told him, "Send them away somewhere else, so that they could look after themselves since **we have nothing to give them".** In verses 13-17, the Lord said, *"That's not true, give them food to eat. You probably don't know it, but you represent the Abundant Kingdom; the inexhaustible Kingdom of God where you don't have to carry a bag in order to have plenty. It is an Abundant Kingdom, where you don't have to have money in order to buy what you want; where you don't have to have fine apparel before you can see the King. It's the kingdom where you don't need a lot to affect cities and nations. The little you have is huge in the hands of God. All you need is faith in God. Preach His kingdom, his rule and reign and heal the sick in every city. That's how you spread the abundance of the Abundant Kingdom."*

Verses 18-20

After all is said and done, in the Abundant Kingdom, you need to know who you are. Most importantly, the Lord says: *"You need to know who I am. Even when you've heard so many theories and doctrines about Me, you need to know for yourself who I am in order to be my true disciple. It is possible that you may be following me around and not even know who I am."*

That is the same way many bear the name "Christian" and attend church services without knowing who the Christ really is.

As he asked the question, Peter answered, *"You are the Christ of God."*

In other words,

*"You are the Anointed One, the Expected One, the Son of God. It was prophesied that you would come to reactivate the kingdom of God, heal the sick and mend the broken hearted. You are the Lord, you are the Master and you are here now. We are your servant. What a privilege to join with you to bring The Abundant Kingdom of God to our generation."*

You might think, "What a question!" Even someone in kindergarten should be able to answer that question, how much more his disciples. Everyone should know that he was the Messiah. You would think so, wouldn't you?

Right from the writings of Moses, the Jews had always expected a Messiah, a Deliverer. No matter what they had been through—oppression, captivity and even exile—they had always expected the appearance of the prophesied Deliverer. They knew He would come and *where* to expect Him, but they did not know *when* or *what* he would look like. And over these hundreds of years, many have risen to proclaim themselves as the Messiah. Majority of them got rounded up quickly by the ruling authority, crushed or made to disperse into hiding.

The need for a Messiah was more intense at the time when the Lord Yeshua was physically on earth. But because of previous experiences, there were many sceptics – even though it was widely believed that the spiritual leaders and the scholars of the law should be able to point Him out from the crowd.

So, you can see why He asked the question. The authorities and the general public may have their doubts. They may still be trying to read between the lines in order to ascertain whether he was really the Messiah they had been waiting for or not.

As for some of the Pharisees and Scholars, there was nothing more to decipher; He was certainly not the Messiah.

"If he was the Christ, why had he not gone after the Romans, to defeat them and set the children of Abraham free? Instead, he has been associating with sinners, women, children and a bunch of uneducated Galileans; he has occupied himself with cheap healing tricks, the feeding of hungry people and controversial raising of "dead" people. He has made us look like fools among the people. That's not how to deliver a people, is it?'

At that time there were various schools of thought as to who and how the Messiah should be. Each opposing view still had great expectation, looking out and looking forward to the day that the Expected One would arrive. They were busy looking forward to the day the picture in their minds would appear, that they did not acknowledge and receive the Lord Yeshua when He started his "deliverance" ministry. Even today, as you read this, some are still seeking the deliverer that occupies the picture in their minds. Invariably, they are missing out on the true Deliverer.

You can understand, then, why Yeshua had to ask His followers who they thought He was; just in case they had no clue who He was! But even after such a Holy Ghost revealed answer from Peter, do you think that Peter, including the other disciples or anyone else there at that time believed in that revelation? What they had been through in their lives had clouded their minds.

What about you; if you were one of the disciples, do you think you would catch on quickly or that you would be different? I have asked myself the same question. I think we would have been the same as the disciples.

They believed that He was the Messiah but still expected Him to one day get up and be a "proper Messiah" who can sack the Romans. As a matter of fact, what we are enjoying now is the benefit of hindsight. We are enjoying the fact that lots of water has passed under the bridge. In other words, many things have been written down, explained and laid bare for us. Even at that, there is still a huge amount that we don't understand.

The disciples didn't have the benefit of the complete New Testament, whether in Greek, Latin, English or in any native language; whether they be authorised or non–authorised, revised or not-so-revised, annotated, abridged, or amplified, the old living and the new living. We have them all, yet we lack in vigour and fruit compared to the work the disciples did with what they had.

As stated earlier, Charles Emeka wrote, *"The issues and battles of life are won and lost in the mind."* The disciples had endured a lot of issues and battles in their lives. Those issues and battles were still lodged in their minds when the Lord asked them that question. Peter answered the question correctly but none of them fully understood the full implication of that answer, not until after His resurrection.

After Yeshua rose from the dead, the eyes of the disciples' inner minds were opened not only to the reality of the fact that the Lord Yeshua was the Messiah but also the *kind* of Messiah he was. That day was the beginning of the renewing of their minds. They knew that they knew, and there was no doubt any more that they knew who the Messiah was. They became willing from then on, specifically from the day of Pentecost, to put their lives on the line and to die for the One who had died for them, the King of kings who rules in the Abundant Kingdom.

# OTHER BOOKS
# BY THIS AUTHOR

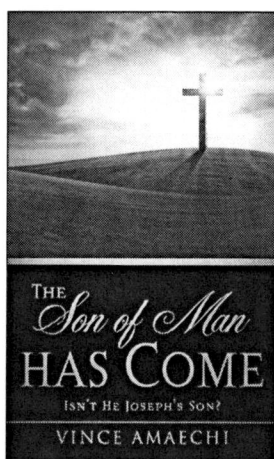

Lightning Source UK Ltd.
Milton Keynes UK
UKOW052134280613

212946UK00001B/4/P